Christian Jr./Sr High School
2100 Greenfield Dr
El Cajon, CA 92019

WITH PASTORAL COMPASSION and biblical clarity, my friend Erwin Lutzer has issued a compelling challenge to God's people, calling us to respond in love and truth to one of the most pressing issues of our time.

—*Joseph M. Stowell*
President, Moody Bible Institute

WITH THE MIND OF A SCHOLAR and the heart of a pastor, Erwin Lutzer has in succinct fashion called evangelicals to stringent but loving action before it is too late for our country. This is the book that should be in the hands of every church member.

—*Paige Patterson*
President, Southwestern Baptist Theological Seminary

THIS BOOK DELIVERS WHAT IT PROMISES: It orients biblical Christians to what they must know about the growing acceptance of and push for the legal establishment of same-sex marriage. Dr. Lutzer documents the teaching of the Bible about homosexual practice, discusses the strategies that have so dramatically boosted acceptance of homosexual lifestyles today, responds to the most common challenges to the moral teachings of the Bible, and offers wise advice on the Church's response to same-sex marriage. Balancing love with a commitment to God's moral will and revealed truth, Lutzer frames the issues correctly and then rightly calls on the Church to rise and be heard on this foundational issue.

—*Stanton L. Jones, Ph.D.*
Provost, Wheaton College
Co-author of Homosexuality: The Use of
ific Research in the Church's Moral Debate

D0018055

I WHOLEHEARTEDLY RECOMMEND THIS BOOK. It presents an intelligent and clear discussion of the true ramifications of same-sex marriages. This insightful and compelling resource will prepare and equip you so that you can properly address this very controversial subject.

—*Sheila Bailey*
International Speaker and wife of the late E. K. Bailey

DR. LUTZER'S FIRST-RATE book makes a compelling addition in the debate. No vital social issue can be settled without first having a thorough understanding of the facts—of what "is"— and then, sitting down together at the table for a good discussion of "what ought to be." As he notes, this is not about hate—it's about debate. The Judeo-Christian argument for traditional marriage rings true because it aligns us with our "manufacturer's" design.

—*Joseph Nicolosi, Ph.D.*
President, NARTH
(National Association of Research and Therapy of Homosexuality)
Author of **Reparative Therapy of Male Homosexuality**
and **A Parent's Guide to Preventing Homosexuality**

THE ISSUE OF SAME-SEX MARRIAGE is one of the most critical of our times. The future of our nation is at stake. That is why I am grateful that Dr. Erwin Lutzer has responded in a biblical way to this vital subject. For Christians looking for answers from God's Word, this book, written by one of our most effective pastors, teachers, and communicators, is required reading.

—*Jack Graham*
President, Southern Baptist Convention
Pastor, Prestonwood Baptist Church

THIS IS A MUST READ for every individual who is concerned about providing a secure future for our children and grandchildren. Lutzer is direct but compassionate, intensely biblical but culturally perceptive. He is also theologically balanced and avoids emotional, reactionary solutions to a problem that—if not corrected—will cause our nation to implode. This book will also provide pastors and teachers with an excellent resource for addressing this crisis in our culture with knowledge, wisdom, and sensitivity.

—*Gene A. Getz*
Pastor Emeritus, Fellowship Bible Church North
Director, The Center for Church Renewal

I COMMEND DR. LUTZER for addressing a difficult topic with truthful love. The battle for same-sex "marriage" does affect you, as well as our society's very future. We must not turn a blind eye to this issue; it is the single greatest threat to religious freedom today.

—*Alan E. Sears*
President, CEO & General Counsel
Alliance Defense Fund

THE NORMALIZATION OF HOMOSEXUALITY through marriage or similar unions is a greater threat to our futures than most are willing to admit or even discuss. Someone must speak out and Dr. Lutzer has done so. Brilliantly.

—*Sandy Rios*
Radio Talk Show Host
Past President, Concerned Women for America

A STRATEGIC BOOK at a pivotal time for the family!

—*Dennis Rainey*
President, FamilyLife

ERWIN LUTZER WRITES WITH THE PASSION of a prophet and the heart of a pastor as he calls upon every Christian to help recover the biblical portrait of marriage and sexuality. America is being threatened by the subversive redefinitions of an immoral subculture seeking to take possession of the next generation. Lutzer writes with compassion and not condemnation as he reveals the dangers of same-sex marriages for the family and the culture as a whole. Every Christian should read this book!

—*Mark L. Bailey*
President, Dallas Theological Seminary

A RIVETING CALL TO ARMS! Erwin Lutzer is challenging the Christian to take a stand in a loving yet non-compromising way. With a vision for the future and knowledge of the past, Lutzer shows the importance of the covenantal marriage between one man and one woman. A crucial read for anyone.

—*Reverend John J. Smid*
Executive Director, Love in Action

AN EXCELLENT BOOK FOR PASTORS AND CHURCH LEADERS to use as they encourage their congregations to adopt a biblically balanced approach to this emotionally charged subject. Dr. Lutzer strikes the right balance between grace and truth in this insightful and practical book. I will recommend it in my circle of influence!

—*William J. Hamel*
President, Evangelical Free Church of America

The Truth About Same-Sex Marriage

6 Things You Need to Know About What's Really at Stake

T 21134

ERWIN W. LUTZER

Christian Jr./Sr High School
2100 Greenfield Dr
El Cajon, CA 92019

MOODY PUBLISHERS
CHICAGO

© 2004 by ERWIN W. LUTZER

All rights reserved. No part of this book may be reproduced in
any form without permission in writing from the publisher,
except in the case of brief quotations embodied in critical
articles or reviews.

All Scripture quotations, unless otherwise indicated, are taken
from the *Holy Bible, New International Version*®. NIV®.
Copyright © 1973, 1978, 1984 by International Bible Society.
Used by permission of Zondervan Publishing House.
All rights reserved.

Scripture quotations marked KJV are taken from the
King James Version.

ISBN: 0-8024-9176-6

Library of Congress
Cataloging-in-Publication Data available

1 3 5 7 9 10 8 6 4 2

Printed in the United States of America

Contents

From My
Heart
to Yours

YOU HOLD IN YOUR HANDS a book that is a reflection of both my love for the homosexual community as well as my deep concern for our nation if same-sex marriages are legalized. When I saw the jubilation of the same-sex couples who were "married," I knew that we as a church had to respond. But, quite frankly, I did not know what to say and do. Two thoughts came immediately to mind: First, I knew that we as a church must have some response both to our political leaders and to the gay community. But on the other hand, I thought it might be too late and reasoned, "Whatever will be, will be."

I quickly learned that many believers simply did not know where they stood on this issue. Some thought that we might as well let homosexuals marry, because what they wanted to do was up to them and it would not bother us; they could live in their world and we could just live in ours. Others thought that since the divorce rate among heterosexuals was so high, we simply did not have the right to sit in judgment upon the gay community.

As I began to study the implications of what same-sex marriages would mean for the wider society, I realized that we were on the verge of the destruction of marriage as we know it. This redefinition of marriage would impact the kind of future we leave for our children and grandchildren. Enormous implications are at stake for us as a nation.

There are also great implications for the church. For, as we shall see in a future chapter of this book, same-sex marriages will jeopardize freedom of religion. A lesbian attorney in Canada correctly said that the real battle is between gay rights and religious freedom; freedom of religion, she said, will have to give way to the homosexual agenda. What is true for Canada applies to the United States.

Most of all, I thought of the young people in our churches who are growing up sexually confused as they are daily exposed to the pro-homosexual pressure of our culture. I wondered what messages same-sex marriages would communicate to them—what would same-sex marriage tell them about marriage, parenting, and role models? At that point I knew we had to speak to this issue.

Finally, I had to ask: *What does God think?* Of course we know that the Bible condemns homosexuality, but I was wondering what God was saying to us as a church through the possibility of this frightening reordering of society. In other words, I was asking God not just for wisdom on how to respond to the culture, but what all of this should mean for His people.

How have we as a church contributed to a cultural vacuum that would allow this redefinition of the family to happen with so little resistance?

Let no one say that we have to choose between loving homosexuals and opposing same-sex marriages. Biblically, love is defined not as license to legitimatize sinful behavior of any kind, but love helps us see that there is a better way. Obviously, we must be as concerned about our own sins as we are about the sins of the homosexual community. We must be concerned enough to speak out about any action, heterosexual or homosexual, that violates God's intended plan for marriage and the family.

I offer you this book from my heart to yours, inviting you to join me in asking God for wisdom as we face our present challenge. Together we can make a difference.

—Erwin W. Lutzer

While We Were Sleeping. . .

*Almost any behavior begins to look
normal if you are exposed to enough of it.*

—MARSHALL KIRK AND HUNTER MADSEN,
GAY ACTIVISTS

HOW DID THINGS GET TO THIS POINT?

Mayor Richard M. Daley of Chicago is widely known as a devoted family man and committed Roman Catholic. Yet, commenting on the rash of homosexual "marriages" being performed by judges openly flouting the law, he stated he would have "no problem" if gay marriages were performed at his City Hall. Daley, an astute politician, can read polls. He knew he could speak out on behalf of same-sex marriage without any fear of political backlash. And the fact that he could do so is a disturbing commentary on our times and on the cultural climate we're living in.

And, perhaps, it's a disturbing commentary on *us*. Because, even though the majority of polls consistently show strong opposition to legalizing gay marriage, such opposition is tepid—and the mayor knows it. He could count on churches, whether Catholic or Protestant, to roll over and play dead.

In the face of what is arguably the most damaging social experiment to ever be attempted in this country, the voices of many are silent—*or have been silenced*, as we shall see.

No more. If ever there was a moment for the church to be the church, it is now.

Before our eyes, we are witnessing a cultural revolution that, if successful, will have ongoing repercussions for our children, our grandchildren and ourselves. There is reason to believe that this revolution to remake the family has the potential to destroy the very concept of marriage along with freedom of religion. If God's people do not act now, it might be too late.

YES, THE BIBLE DOES CONDEMN HOMOSEXUALITY, BUT IT ALSO CONDEMNS A HOST OF OTHER SINS THAT ARE RAMPANT IN THE BEST OF OUR CHURCHES.

When four justices in a Massachusetts courtroom ruled, with what some have called an astonishing act of self-righteousness, that it was unconstitutional to bar homosexuals from marriage, they set in motion a series of dominoes that no one—not even the gays themselves—could have predicted. In courtrooms throughout different parts of the country, judges conducted ceremonies "marrying" jubilant homosexuals—people like lesbian Laura Bauer, who was wed to her partner of eight years in a February ceremony in San Francisco. "This is a great thing for us," she said. "With everyone talking about family, now we can give our daughter a family, and no one can take that away from us."[1]

Then there's Beth Niernberg. She lives in New York with two male homosexual lovers and together they "co-parent" three boys. Ms. Niernberg stays home and takes care of the boys, while the men, both psychiatrists, go off to work. The boys are each biologically related to Ms. Niernberg and to one of their dads. The trio's agreement includes the proviso that when Ms. Niernberg finds a suitable female partner, the trio will become a quartet.

Meet what *World* magazine calls the "new America," where, reporter Lynn Vincent observes, "public officials are stretching the definition of marriage beyond the historical bonds of blood, adoption and matrimony."[2]

REDEMPTION, NOT RANCOR

We've all heard these stories and seen the images of celebrating homosexuals. We've all been appalled, and justifiably so. But this is no time for self-righteous finger-pointing or impotent hand-wringing. As I hope to show, we all share responsibility for what many properly regard as a frightful social experiment taking place before our eyes. We must respond to this crisis, but *how* we respond is of utmost importance.

The purpose of this book is to encourage and equip God's people to defend marriage, giving reasons why its definition should not be broadened to include same-sex marriages. But here I must emphasize that first and foremost this book aims at *redemption*, not rancor. We must lower our voices in this debate, speaking with respect and dignity. No matter how strongly we oppose the homosexual agenda, we are first of all called to be Christians who have the privilege of representing Christ to all the communities of the world, regardless of class, color, nationality or "gender orientation."

Second, this is a book written with the same compassion for the gay community that we should have for all who share this hurting planet. We must never speak of homosexuality as if it is the one sin worthy of the eternal flames. Yes, the Bible does condemn homosexuality, but it also condemns a host of other sins that are rampant in the best of our churches. If all we do is shout at homosexuals across a chasm, be assured we will hear only the echo of our own voice ringing in the air.

We've all known families with gay children, whether sons or daughters. I recall one man who was quick to denounce homosexuality, and then discovered to his everlasting chagrin that his own son was gay. Rather than repenting of his self-righteous attitude, this father, in what he deemed to be a grand show of consistency, disinherited his son, telling him he was no longer welcome at home. Of course the father was right in disagreeing with his son's lifestyle, but quite wrong in his response to his own flesh and blood. We should not be surprised that his son flaunted his "gayness" and became a leader in the homosexual movement.

I am under no illusion that the radical gay community will listen to what we have to say. For reasons, some of which may be of our own making, they have turned a deaf ear to the church. But, I also believe that there are thousands of other gays who are still listening, waiting to hear from the church a word of understanding, direction, and hope.

Third, this is a book written primarily for the church—that is, those of us who, because of our allegiance to Jesus Christ, oppose same-sex unions, but struggle with the question of how that opposition is best expressed. The task at hand is to help us understand the basis for our convictions and what should be done with what we believe. It is not enough to condemn the darkness, if we fail to shine a light of hope on our disintegrating culture.

How We Got Here

Before we can look at "where we go from here," we must look at how we got to this point—seemingly while we in the church were sleeping. The story of how approximately 2 percent of the population has been able to impose its agenda on America and marginalize all opposition is one that can only be briefly summarized here—but it is a story we cannot afford to ignore.

The story begins in the 1960s—ironically, with heterosexuals. The invention of the Pill and the general loosening of societal mores and insistence on "rights" in various spheres spawned a revolution in sexual attitudes. Sexual self-expression, which traditionally had been regarded as a privilege, became perceived as a right—something to be expressed publicly, frequently, and outside of monogamous, lifelong marriage. The consensus that "good girls don't" (and neither do boys) eroded. Of course, promiscuity has always been with us, but previous generations shared an understanding that although sex outside of marriage happened, it should not be so.

With the onslaught of pornography, the Playboy philosophy steadily shifted the center of gravity from marital faithfulness to personal enjoyment. Thus, if your mate no longer fulfilled your needs, you should have the "right" to find someone who would. To quote Lynn Vincent in *World*, "Cohabitation began shedding its stigma, leading to a revolving door family structure that often left children fatherless and economically deprived."[3]

With divorce available for the sake of convenience, the word *family* began to take on new meanings. Now it was common for a mother to raise the children alone, or possibly with a new husband—or at least a new lover. Meanwhile, the husband and father went off to pursue his own relationships which he deemed "best" for him. Children reared without their father's love and protection became vulnerable to sexual experimentation and abuse.

Gradually, the notion of a family with a father, mother and children, all living under the same roof, became something of a relic of a bygone era, at least in some quarters. Our associate pastor here at the Moody Church reminded us of this when he told of a stroll his family took in Lincoln Park, just north of the church. As he and his wife and four children walked along the sidewalk, one elderly lady, sitting on a park bench next to her friend, said, "Look! A family!" No doubt she hadn't seen "a family" for a long while!

Meanwhile, *tolerance* emerged as the one indisputable national value. This word, which at one time meant that people should be free to *believe* whatever they wished, now meant that they could *do* whatever they wished, and it was improper to judge their conduct. Tolerance now demands an affirmation of virtually all behavior, no matter how immoral, unnatural, and bizarre. With these streams flowing into our national culture, much of America was ready for same-sex marriages.

THE STRATEGY THAT WORKED

For more than thirty years, gay activists have intentionally sought to make their lifestyle and behavior "normal" in the eyes of mainstream America. In 1973, activists persuaded the

American Psychiatric Association to remove homosexuality from its list of psychiatric illnesses and reclassify it as normal behavior. This change was made, not because of scientific data but because radicals planned a systematic effort to disrupt the annual meetings of the APA.

Three years earlier, activists grabbed the microphone in an APA meeting and said, "Psychiatry is the enemy incarnate. Psychiatry has waged a relentless war of extermination against us. You may take this as a declaration of war against you . . . we're rejecting you all as our owners."[4] One prominent psychiatrist said it was the first time in psychiatric history that a scientific society ignored scientific evidence and yielded to the demands of a militant group.[5]

Through this action, the radical gay movement let it be known that its agenda would proceed regardless of research, science, and dialogue; and that intimidation would be one of its weapons to achieve its aims, no matter what.

Consider the game plan put forward by two gay activists, Marshall Kirk and Hunter Madsen, and publicized in a 1987 article titled "The Overhauling of Straight America" and a 1989 book titled *After the Ball*.

Both are quoted and referred to extensively in the excellent book *The Homosexual Agenda*, by Alan Sears and Craig Osten. Here are some of the details of how the gay establishment plans to change American attitudes about homosexuality.

First, they say, homosexuals should talk about gays and gayness as loudly and as often as possible. They write, ". . . almost all behavior begins to look normal if you are exposed to enough of it at close quarters and among your acquaintances."[6] Certainly we would agree that the media have cooperated with this strategy. Sitcoms, movies, and documentaries are calculated to make the practice of homosexuality seem normal. With this barrage of media hype, we either are forced to accept their behavior as normal, or we become sick of it and withdraw from the cultural debate.

Thus the radical homosexuals with their savvy cooperation with a willing media keep pushing on society as much as it will tolerate. Yes, history has shown that it is true that "almost all behavior begins to look normal if you are exposed to enough of it at close quarters and among your acquaintances."

Second, the homosexual authors write, "Portray gays as victims, not aggressive challengers"—a strategy designed to play to most Americans' sympathy for the underdog. So the homosexual community has intentionally portrayed themselves as a victimized class in need of special protection. To continue in their words, "A media campaign that casts gays as society's victims and encourages straights to be their protectors must make it easier for those who respond to assert that and explain their new perspectives."[7] The media have obliged; in fact, it is not too strong to say that promoting the gay agenda is high on the list of priorities for those who bring us our news and entertainment.

When a young homosexual, Mathew Shepard, was murdered, many gays and members of the media turned his brutal killing into an opportunity to blame his death on all those who oppose the gay agenda. James Dobson of Focus on the Family bore much of the wrath of the targeted media campaign. Deborah Mathis, writing in the *Orlando Sentinel*, commented:

> The opponents of homosexual behavior prefer not to acknowledge their own bigotry. Hence, the disguise—or self-delusion—of noble purpose . . . Did the antihomo-

sexual crowd help kill Mathew Shepard? Not per se. But it poisoned the air, which poisoned the minds which connived to attract, deceive and destroy a young man who deserved, in the least, to be left alone. They share in the complicity.[8]

She went on to liken conservative Christians to Adolf Hitler.

So there you have it: A homosexual was murdered, and it is the fault of all those who are not in step with the homosexual agenda. No matter that Mathew Shepard was killed by irreligious drunken thugs. The media gave the gay community wide and continuous support, propagating the myth that Christians who speak out against the homosexual agenda were to blame for the murder.

Third, they say that it is important to make the gays look good and their victims look bad. This is done by convincing the public that many famous people in history were gay, and, of course, that gays must consistently be portrayed favorably in the media. The authors write, "We intend to make the antigays look so nasty that average Americans will want to disassociate themselves from such types."[9]

Perhaps I should pause here to say that sadly, some "antigays" do look nasty. The media frequently gives attention to one man, who on occasion attends gay events carrying his sign, "God Hates Fags." Whatever his motivation, he has given gays the opportunity to paint those of us who oppose their agenda with the same brush. Conservative churches are often portrayed as hateful, homophobic, and nasty. The caricature works.

Fourth, the authors suggest a plan that has become wildly successful: to solicit money from corporations to promote homosexuality and neutralize all opposition to the lifestyle. For example the Ford Foundation has provided grants to the National Gay and Lesbian Task Force Policy Institute and the Lambda Legal Defense and Education Fund which lobbies for same-sex marriage.[10] This Lambda Legal Defense Fund also claims to have received support from IBM and United Airlines.

WE CANNOT LIST HERE ALL OF THE ADVANCES OF THE GAY AGENDA, EXCEPT TO SAY THAT VIRTU- ALLY EVERYTHING THEY HAVE WANTED HAS COME TO PASS.

In their book, Kirk and Madsen speak about the skillful use of propaganda that must be used to "overhaul straight America." They write that homosexuals must always be portrayed in a positive light, and then they add, "It makes no difference that the ads [portraying homosexuals as icons of normality] are lies, not to us . . . nor to bigots."[11]

Eric Pollard, the founder of ACT-UP, a militant homosexual group, writes that lying was a part of the strategy of the activists, referencing Adolf Hitler as a model to follow. He writes, "By clever and persevering use of propaganda, even heaven can be represented as hell to the people, and conversely, the most wretched life as paradise."[12]

The strategy has worked. We cannot list here all of the advances of the gay agenda, except to say that virtually everything they have wanted has come to pass. In the years since then, sex education in the public schools has promoted homosexuality. In 2001, the National Educational Association adopted resolutions to promote the full-scale indoctrination of children to accept and affirm homosexual behavior. When word leaked out of their intentions, they "tabled" the motion, which means that they will quietly implement it without official member approval.[13] No dissenting views are allowed; parents are silenced and children encouraged to experiment with various forms of sexual behavior.

Laws against discrimination in the workplace are now upheld, and the word *tolerance* now means that one must endorse homosexual behavior. Even the Boy Scouts have been marginalized because they have resisted having homosexuals as leaders and they have retained the word *God* in their pledge. Never mind that most parents do not want homosexuals to be teaching and leading their boys, never mind that the word *God* is still in our nation's Pledge of Allegiance. With cynical disdain, the radical arm of the homosexual movement has done all they can to shut down all funding for the Scouts, a beloved organization that has played such a positive role in shaping the characters of many boys and men.

Many of us have watched the gains of the gay movement with great concern. But now we can no longer simply watch. With the possibility that the definition of marriage will include same-sex marriages, we must ask: What can we do at this late hour? And if we cannot change the present, what are we doing to change the future?

Whatever your views on the subject, I invite you to read this book with a spirit of discernment and compassion. When you are finished I hope you will agree that there are compelling reasons to reject the redefinition of marriage and the family. I also hope you will do your part in standing against this cultural phenomenon and the implications such a change in our attitudes and laws would bring. This is no time for name-calling and intimidation. It is a time for rational discussion and thoughtful reflection.

My final request is that you read this book to the end. To read one chapter or one paragraph is to miss a part of the framework in which this battle is fought. We must try to listen to each other with humility and care.

The kind of society we have for our children and grandchildren is at stake.

The Church
Must Speak

1

As marriage becomes unnecessary, the whole nation will be "living in sin."

—Gene Edward Veith

"What difference does it make to me?" one man asked when interviewed about same-sex marriages. "It won't affect the way I love my wife and kids."

Is it true that same-sex marriages can take place in one part of our society and not affect "the rest of us"? Is this just one more of those issues that we should learn to tolerate in a free and open society?

Imagine that you are on a large boat, hoping to get to the other side of a lake, when one man insists that he has a "right" to drill a hole through the bottom of *his* side of the boat. When you object, he argues for tolerance, and reminds you that you can just stay on your side with *your* friends; what he does on his side has no bearing on what you do on your side. But as the water begins to seep into the boat, you are suddenly aware, that, like it or not, what one person does on his side of the boat affects everyone in the boat.

We cannot be content to rest secure in our evangelical enclaves. As we saw in the previous introduction, some very smart homosexual activists have spent the last several decades energetically and methodically remaking American attitudes toward what was formerly broadly considered a deviant behavior. These activists have seized the agenda and control the national conversation, putting those who care about marriage and family—and how it has been understood for centuries—on the defensive.

We need, therefore, to understand and respond. And there are three reasons why the church cannot be silent.

WHAT IS A "FAMILY"?

So why should we be worried? First, we need to realize that in some quarters a concentrated push to "reinvent" the family is under way. For example, the San Francisco Unified School District has a lesson plan for teaching kindergarteners and first graders about homosexuality. It defines a family as a "unit of two or more persons, related either by birth or by choice, who may or may not live together, who try to meet each other's needs and share common goals and interests . . . "[1] Gone is the idea that a family should include a mother and a father in a committed relationship rearing their children. Consonant with the notion that "I and only I define what's best for me," we are witnessing an effort to redefine *family*. And, because of the prevalence of divorce, serial marriages, and cohabitation, the effort is pretty effective.

If we want to find out what would happen if same-sex marriages become law, we need only take a look at what is happening in some countries of Europe, where such legislation already exists. The answer, in brief, is that the change in laws has, in effect, wrought the destruction of marriage. For example, in France, "civil solidarity pacts" have been created for homosexuals so that they can file joint income tax returns and receive welfare and unemployment benefits. Obviously, such an arrangement had to be made available to everyone, including cohabiting heterosexual couples, to widowed sisters, even to priests and their housekeepers.

Because these "pacts" are easier to enter and easier to exit, and impose fewer legal obligations, many heterosexual couples enter into these agreements rather than becoming married. If these couples think that these "pacts" provide a stable home environment for children, they should keep in mind that the average cohabitational relationship lasts about five years. David Frum writes, "Apologists for cohabitation praise it as a less burdensome alternative to marriage; the truth is that it is a near-certain prelude to fatherlessness."[2]

He continues: "The argument over gay marriage is only incidentally and secondarily an argument over gays. What it is first and fundamentally is an argument over marriage. . . . gay marriage will turn out in practice to mean the creation of an alternative form of legal coupling that will be available to homosexual and heterosexuals alike. Gay marriage, as the French are vividly demonstrating, does not extend marital rights; it abolishes marriage and puts a new, flimsier institution in its place."[3]

Consider: If marriage is no longer the union of one man and one woman but rather any two persons who want to cohabit, who is to say that it must be limited to two people? Why not a trio of three men or women? And why not one man with two wives or ten? After all, we must extend "equal rights" to all individuals to live according to any arrangement they wish. The end result is the destruction of marriage as we know it—with children the losers.

A conference at the University of London called "Legal Recognition of Same-Sex Marriage: A Conference on National European and International Law" explored the question of whether marriage should exist at all. They discussed strategies on how to bypass each nation's democratic process and use the judicial process to sanction same-sex marriages. They also discussed how adults could be free to pursue any sexual relationship they want, with no legal restrictions whatsoever.[4]

Gene Edward Veith, writing in *World* magazine, summed up the consequences for our society if marriage is redefined:

> Under the emerging framework, there will be no difference between a married couple, a homosexual couple, or a couple in a temporary sexual relationship. As many advocates are putting it, "What difference does it make to the government or an employer whom you are having sex with?"
>
> This sort of reductionism—a spouse is nothing more than a sex partner, so a sex partner is the same as a spouse—misses the point of what marriage is and what its role in society amounts to . . . as marriage becomes unnecessary—not just for job benefits but for adopting children, inheriting property, and being socially acceptable—the whole nation will be "living in sin."[5]

No one knows better than the homosexuals themselves as to what same-sex marriages will mean for society as a whole.

Evan Wolfson, former president of the Lambda Legal Defense and Educational Fund, a gay advocacy group, writes, "We can win the freedom to marry . . . We can seize the terms of the debate, tell our diverse stories, engage the nongay persuadable public, enlist allies, work the courts and the legislatures in several states, and achieve a legal breakthrough with five years . . . This won't just be a change in the law either; it will be a change in society. For if we do it right, the struggle to win the freedom to marry will being much more along the way . . ."[6]

That "much more along the way" goes far beyond the cozy media portrayals of Norman Rockwell-like gay parents and kids—which is where many good church people stop. George Dent, writing in *The Journal of Law and Politics*, says that once same-sex marriage is affirmed, then other forms of "marriage" will quickly be affirmed as well, such as polygamy, endogamy (the marriage of blood relatives) and child marriage. In fact, the policy guide of the American Civil Liberties Union calls for the legalization of polygamy, stating, "The ACLU believes that criminal and civil laws prohibiting or penalizing the practice of plural marriage violate constitutional protections for freedom of expression and association, freedom of religion, and privacy for personal relationships among consenting adults."[7] After all, who is to tell adults how many partners they should have, if they have equal rights under the constitution?

> IF MARRIAGE IS NO LONGER THE UNION OF ONE MAN AND ONE WOMAN, WHO IS TO SAY IT MUST BE LIMITED TO TWO PEOPLE?

Part of the strategy of deception undertaken by gays has been to try to convince straight America that they, the gays, are just like us, except that rather than John and Jane, they come together as John and John or Jane and Jane. The seamier aspects of the lifestyle—the bars, the disease, the cruising, the truly perverted practices—are intentionally downplayed. We will look at homosexual sexuality in an upcoming chapter. But listen to homosexual author Andrew Sullivan (a political conservative and professing Catholic). He says that most homosexuals understand that sexual commitment in a marriage "is much broader than what nearly all heterosexual couples will tolerate." Homosexuals, he says, have a "need for extramarital outlets" and therefore same-sex marriage will make adultery more acceptable for all married couples.[8]

This battle is not just about the desire of some gays and lesbians to be left alone to live peaceful lives and to be able to "love" like the rest of us. It is not simply about the need for one partner to receive health-insurance benefits from the other's work. Once the wheels are set in motion, our society will be on a road to a dark and unthinkable future.

WHEN TRUTH BECOMES "HATE SPEECH"

You sit in your church on a Sunday, listening to your pastor. You follow along in your Bible and take notes as he speaks on some issue relevant to your life and to our culture. Surrounded by believers and seekers, you are content.

This Lord's Day picture is a cherished part of the lives of tens of millions in this land. Yet, should same-sex marriage come to pass in this country, this freedom you and I now possess under the Bill of Rights could conceivably be imperiled.

There are many ways that the radical homosexuals have tried to silence the church. One is by publicizing support for gays by more moderate church leaders who speak favorably of the gay agenda. This is intended to raise questions in the minds of those who take the Bible as God's Word and therefore see homosexuality as an unnatural act. If a part of the church can support gay marriages, why should others oppose it? If main-stream Christianity agrees with them, it is just those "wacky fundamentalists" who are out of step with the gay agenda. So the "radical right," as it is called, is painted as bigoted, intolerant, and hateful—because, as we all know, Jesus supposedly welcomes all and judges none.

We've heard much about hate-speech legislation, which is intended to force us to keep our convictions to ourselves. An assistant state's attorney told me that until now the church has had a niche where freedom of religion can be exercised. But if and when same-sex marriage becomes a reality, churches that refuse to perform such unions will find that their tax-exempt status will soon be revoked. He predicts endless lawsuits that will bankrupt many churches.

The homosexual lobby is not content with "separate but equal." In the words of Joel Belz, "It [the homosexual lobby] seeks instead to ensure that everyone else in society also engages in that behavior or at least gives it tacit approval."[9] He goes on to remind his readers that the California Supreme Court ruled by a 6-1 margin that the Catholic Charities

WHEN SAME-SEX MARRIAGES ARE LEGALIZED, RELIGIOUS FREEDOM WILL HAVE TO GIVE WAY TO CONSTITUTIONAL LAW.

organization is required to provide health insurance for forms of birth control that Catholic Charities finds morally objectionable. In other words, everyone has to do what the minority wants the privilege of doing. Then, Belz adds this, "Nor is it unthinkable in such a climate that courts will soon rule that *World* magazine, and other organizations like us, will be required to hire employees—including editorial writers—who are ardent proponents of same-sex marriage, and of course, who have already entered such relationships."[10]

Note it well: when same-sex marriages are legalized, religious freedom will have to give way to constitutional law. We can hear it already: "All people have a constitutional right to marriage, in whatever gender arrangement they desire; the church, therefore, is breaking the law in denying people their constitutionally guaranteed rights."

As far back as 1994, a gay activist proposed a change in policy of the American Psychiatric Association that would make it a violation of professional conduct for a psychiatrist to help a homosexual out of the lifestyle, *even at the patient's request*.[11] This in spite of the fact that one of the association's own professional standards holds that psychiatrists need to accept a patient's own goals in treatment. Only when objectors threatened a lawsuit against the APA, forcing it to reopen the decision of 1973 that redefined homosexuality as normal— only with such a threat did the activists back down.

But the point for our interest is that this gay task force made clear that it not only wanted to prevent psychiatrists from those therapies that would lead homosexuals out of the lifestyle, but they also had in mind social workers, counselors, and pastors.[12] If same-sex marriages were legal and homosexuality were in all respects given the same status as heterosexuality, the argument could be made that it is both prejudicial and contrary to existing laws of equality to help someone change from one sexual orientation to another. Such help implies that one orientation is better than other, which some will protest as hateful and bigoted.

The Canadian experience is instructive. Hate speech legislation, intended to silence the church, is already law in Canada where one cannot speak against homosexuality in the media; heavy fines are levied if one says that homosexuality is a sin. Indeed, Focus on the Family has had programs taken off the air in Canada because they were deemed "hate speech."

In Canada, Bill C-250, which is on the brink of becoming law, would make public criticism of homosexuality a crime. The Saskatchewan Human Rights Commission ruled that a newspaper ad listing passages that oppose homosexuality was a human-rights offense. The paper and the man who placed the ad each had to pay three homosexual men $1,500, because they objected to it. In British Columbia a teacher who wrote a letter to the newspaper saying that homosexuality was not a fixed orientation was suspended.[13]

Please don't misunderstand: Even if freedom of religion is taken away from us, the church will continue to fulfill its responsibility of representing Jesus Christ in the world. Study church history and you'll discover that almost always the church has had to cope in a hostile culture with virtually no freedom. Repeatedly, the church has proved that it does not need freedom to survive. Ultimately the church is in the hands of Jesus—not the ACLU.

In the meantime, the "mainstream" media continue to demonstrate astonishing bias against orthodox believers—bias that would not be tolerated against gays themselves. In my own city, newspaper columnist Richard Roeper wrote an opinion piece critical of President Bush's announcement supporting a constitutional amendment banning same-sex marriages. He sarcastically wrote,

> Thank God for Bush's stance in favor of constitutional amendment banning gay marriage. Because of course, God hates the gays. And we can't go around legitimizing their depravity, or God might come to hate us too.[14]

He mocked the phrase "sanctity of marriage" and the idea that it should apply to heterosexuals only. He described "hundreds of gay couples joyously celebrating their love, and lots of protestors showing up at such ceremonies to voice their loathing of the homosexual lifestyle." He also said that he receives e-mails from people who hate gays.

I wrote a detailed reply, pointing out that his article is a good example of the strategy that is often used to silence opposition to the gay agenda: portray those who are opposed to the imposition of gay values as hatemongers, and portray the gay community as the loving, caring part of our society. Unfortunately, such tactics have intimidated many people who don't want to be branded as hateful and vindictive. I concluded the letter by saying,

> Let those religious people who "hate gays" repent of their sin; let those who foment hate against those of us who oppose gay marriages come to their senses. Those who disagree with what I have written are free to do so. But let them respond with thoughtful respect rather than with the smear tactics that have so often been used

in this controversy. We do after all share this planet with diverse people, and our responsibility is to show love and respect despite our deeply held disagreements.

Interestingly, no part of my letter was printed in the newspaper.

ARE WE MISREADING THE BIBLE?

Many within the radical homosexual movement do not pretend that their lifestyle is consistent with the Bible. But others argue that the church has "misunderstood" what the Bible actually says about homosexuality.

As we know, the Episcopal Church, contrary to its own rules, has ordained an openly gay bishop. Keep in mind that previously he was married to a woman whom he divorced to live with a man in an unmarried relationship. Interestingly, if a divorced man were to live with a woman to whom he was not married, even the most liberal church leaders would probably demur. But, as we have learned, special exceptions are often made for homosexuals because of the perceived prejudice against them. All this is done under the banner of *love*, which supposedly cancels all of the Scripture that condemns the homosexual lifestyle.

IN MATTERS OF SEXUALITY, WE ARE TEMPTED TO FALL INTO THE "MY FEELINGS ARE RIGHT ABOUT THIS, AND GOD HAD BETTER AGREE WITH ME" SYNDROME.

We must point out that the Bible does not speak about homosexuality with a muffled voice. In their book *The Same-Sex Controversy*, authors James R. White and Jeffrey D. Niell do a careful study of all the different methods of interpretation used in a vain attempt to insist that homosexuality is compatible with the Scriptures. They point out that any fair reading of the book of Leviticus proves that God calls homosexuality an "abomination," and these opinions cannot be set aside as we do the dietary and civil codes of the Old Testament. What is more, the New Testament speaks with the same clarity as the Old on the subject.[15]

The strong condemnation of sexual sin in the Bible—whether homosexual or heterosexual—is further proof that we as fallen creatures are prone to deception in matters of sexuality. Here as nowhere else are we often subject to the error of arguing from our passions back to what God must or must not approve. We are tempted to fall into the "My feelings are right about this, and therefore the people around me in general and God in particular, had better agree with me" syndrome.

Let those churches committed to the Scriptures ask themselves: What should our stance be toward same-sex marriages? Can we afford to remain silent? Since God has not been silent on the subject it is difficult for us to justify our own penchant for looking the other way. Yes, the church must speak, but what does it have to say?

WHAT THE CHURCH HAS TO SAY TO THE GAY COMMUNITY

What would we say to the gay community if we were actually granted a hearing? Let's admit that there are many radicals who will not listen; their ears are closed, their hearts are hardened so nothing we say will make a difference. They have dismantled any bridges of communication with those who disagree with them, except to call them names.

But there are others—perhaps a majority—who are in the homosexual lifestyle and would leave it if they thought they could. Their consciences are awakened to the wrongness of what they do, and yet they feel trapped. I believe that we as evangelicals have failed these people, many of whom populate our churches.

As a pastor I've listened to their stories of brokenness and heartache. I've heard stories of molestation, of the emptiness of sex without commitment, without love, without caring. No matter what we see on television, the gay community is hurting, compulsively acting out behavior to cover their pain. These are the people for whom we must have compassion, understanding, and care. It's a hurting world out there, and all of the wells are dry.

Several years ago when I was invited to speak at an Exodus conference (an organization dedicated to helping gays come out of their lifestyle), I was awakened to the pain in the gay community and determined to never speak about homosexuals without compassion and humility. At a breakfast table with four or five lesbians, I learned that 80 percent of all lesbians had been molested or otherwise mistreated by men— often by the father, a baby-sitter, or a stranger. Their hatred for men drove them into same-sex relationships that were difficult to break. To quote the words of one woman who came out of the lifestyle, "If you'd asked me a year ago if I could have come out of the gay movement, it would have been equivalent to asking me to move this building . . . *impossible!*"

So whatever we say must be said with understanding, compassion, love and hope. But because we love and because we care, we must speak.

THE GAYS AMONG US

We must begin speaking of our own sins, the sins we tolerate in our own lives and the lives of our churches. We must repent of the double standard that sees the sin of homosexual behavior in a different category than adultery, premarital sex, and pornography. We must plead guilty to the charge of bigotry, for we have acted as if our sins are minor in comparison to those of the homosexual community, whose sins we think are of a different nature and category. This attitude of condemnation has caused us to lose our voice in the wider culture.

We have an obligation to maintain the biblical standards without wavering, but also speak with a healing and redemptive voice. This we have failed to do.

We must also confess that we have failed to make a distinction between the agenda of the radical gay community and the young people in our churches who might be confused about their gender. Or between the radicals and the son or daughter who has adopted the gay lifestyle, but is looking for a way out.

We have closed our eyes to the fact that there are many gay people in our churches who wish that they could be different, but have been indoctrinated by a culture that insists that no one can change, and therefore a homosexual lifestyle is inevitable. As one homosexual said to me, "This is the card I have been dealt." These are the hurting people we have too often alienated and have not helped. Whatever criticisms I have made of Richard Roeper's article, I am grieved when I hear that people send him e-mails saying they hate gays. Thus the stereotype that all of us do is inevitable.

I've had the experience—as I'm sure you have—where a high-profile religious leader has been interviewed by the press, only to make some extreme statement that does not represent my own convictions. Yet those of us who are evangelical pastors know that we will be painted with the same brush.

So we have to remember that the radical gay community does not speak for all gays. When we read that NAMBLA, the North American Man-Boy Love Association, wants to lower the age of sexual consent to 13, and when we read that a book has been published that advocates sex with children, we must remember that the authors do not speak for all of the homosexual community. Indeed, such writers might speak only for a small fraction of it. If we don't like it when others paint us with a big brush, let's not do the same with the gay community.

THERE ARE MANY YOUNG PEOPLE IN OUR CHURCHES WHO FEAR THEY MIGHT BE GAY AND YET CANNOT TALK TO ANYONE ABOUT IT, EXPECTING REJECTION AND RIDICULE.

In my own ministry, I've always tried to distinguish between the advocates of the radical gay agenda and the gays that attend our services who are seeking help and hope. Our sensitivity antennae must be more finely tuned. There are many young people in our churches who fear they might be gay and yet cannot talk to anyone about it, expecting rejection and ridicule. Thus they suffer alone, managing their sexuality as best they can. Secrecy forces them to become preoccupied with their sexuality, and soon they begin experimentation. We do not help them by singling out homosexuality as the one great sin and then doing double damage by lumping them with the radicals whose agenda we oppose.

To speak plainly, I believe we have failed to properly represent Christ and the gospel in the wider world, including the gay world. We have contributed to the cultural vacuum that has allowed the radicals to establish their turf and promote their demands. When we hear that the television viewing habits of Christians and non-Christians are about the same, is it any wonder that we have lost our voice in society?

We cannot lay all the blame for what is happening at the door of the church, because there are many streams that feed our culture. But we must humbly admit that culture has influenced us more than we have influenced the culture. And worse, we have been content with ourselves, without the hint that we desperately need to be broken before God about our own failures.

Our first word to the homosexual community is that we ourselves need repentance.

WHAT ARE WE TO SAY?

We have to emphasize to the gay community that opposition to same-sex marriages is not about *hate*, but about *debate*. Opposition to what some of us see as a devastating move that will further weaken the family and harm children—such opposition is not hateful. Morality is not bigotry.

In their excellent book, *The Homosexual Agenda*, from which I have already extensively quoted, authors Alan Sears and Craig Osten give this illustration which I've summarized: Imagine that you are standing at the bottom of a cliff and you are watching as someone on the ledge above you is walking backwards, and in a few steps he will surely fall over the precipice. You shout, warning him to stop, and before you know it, a crowd gathers around you, snapping your picture and accusing you of "hate speech." You are being warned to keep your prejudices to yourself. After all, who are you to tell someone where they can and can't walk? Who are you to say that someone can't walk backwards? You are dumbfounded, but there you are, the object of everyone's wrath.[16]

To the skeptics reading this: Just suppose for a moment that the Bible is the Word of God, and this same Word condemns homosexuality. Suppose, furthermore, that God created children to need both a father and a mother to model gender diversity. Suppose that homosexuality in the end is destructive not just to society but to the individual homosexuals themselves. Supposing all the above are true, would it be "hateful" to oppose same-sex marriages?

We believe we are derelict if we allow the pro-gay culture to dictate what we can and can't say; we are shirking our duty if we are silenced because we will be called names and otherwise derided. Is not the Christian faith best seen in the light of false accusations, misunderstanding and being the object of "focused hatred"?

The Church and Forgiveness

Finally, we must send the message that homosexuality is not an unpardonable sin. Neither is adultery, nor even incest. This is why the Bible frequently lists a host of other sins right along with those related to sexuality: "The acts of the sinful nature are obvious: sexual immorality, impurity and debauchery; idolatry and witchcraft; hatred, discord, jealousy, fits of rage, selfish ambition, dissensions, factions and envy; drunkenness, orgies, and the like. I warn you, as I did before, that those who live like this will not inherit the kingdom of God" (Galatians 5:19–21). The list looks like a description of our culture.

To those who are still listening, we must say that at issue is not the greatness of our sin, but the wonder of the righteousness which God credits to those who believe in His Son. It has been correctly said that the ground is level at the foot of the cross. We all come as needy sinners; we all come with the same need for the pardon that God alone can give us.

Visualize two roads. One is rough and rutted; the other smooth and well maintained. Their differences are apparent to all who pass by. But when a blanket of snow comes—let's say twelve inches—then the roads look the very same. Just so, regardless of our past, we urge all who come to Christ, "Come now, let us reason together," says the Lord. "Though your sins are like scarlet they shall be as white as snow; though they are red as crimson, they shall be like wool" (Isaiah 1:18). In the same way, the righteousness of Christ covers us as sinners, and we stand before God without shame and condemnation.

To the person reading this—homosexual or otherwise—I urge you to come to Christ *as you are*. Come to Jesus as a homosexual, as a heterosexual, as a thief, as an alcoholic, but *come*. We come to Jesus as we are, but as someone has said, He loves us too much to leave us that way. Hear His words, "Yet to all who received him, to those who believed in his name, he gave the right to become children of God" (John 1:12).

As we are fond of saying, "There is more grace in God's heart than there is sin in your past." A friend of mine, quoting a Puritan divine, said, "God is a better Savior than you are a sinner."

And yet there is more to be said.

We Must Consult the Designer's Manual

2

Humanity in community is male and female. And one is the full image of God alone.

—WALTER BRUEGGEMANN

WHY DID GOD CREATE MARRIAGE?

The Genesis account of creation gives us the best understanding of what we know about marriage, its meaning and purpose; and what happens when we violate the divine pattern. If we can discern what the Designer had in mind, we are better able to understand what is at stake in our same-sex marriage debate. In the process, we'll discover that a biblical view of sexuality explains the brokenness in our culture as no other book on sex or marriage. Here at last we have answers that ring true to what we know about gender and diversity.

Think of it: Although Adam had the awesome privilege of walking with God in the Garden of Eden, the Lord still said that something important was missing! "It is not good for the man to be alone; I will make him a helper suitable for him"

(Genesis 2:18). God clearly affirms that man is a social creature and needs a companion who is "suitable" for him.

When God created Adam, He chose to use the dust of the ground for the raw material. "Then the LORD God formed man of the dust from the ground, and breathed into his nostrils the breath of life; and man became a living being" (Genesis 2:7).

We might expect God to make a similar form from dust when He created Eve. But we read, "So the LORD God caused the man to fall into a deep sleep; and while he was sleeping, he took one of the man's ribs and closed up the place with flesh. The LORD God made a woman from the rib he had taken out of the man, and he brought her to the man" (Genesis 2:21–22). When God created Eve out of Adam's flesh, He made a powerful statement about our sexuality. God separated femininity out of masculinity, forming two separate people. With this separation came a powerful implanted desire in the male and the female to be reunited in an intimate oneness.

BOTH GENDERS BEAR THE IMAGE OF GOD, THOUGH THEY REFLECT GOD IN DIFFERENT WAYS.

Femininity and masculinity would now lie at the heart of who we are as people. Our sexual desires are rooted in creation, proof that sex was created by God as an expression of unity and love between a man and a woman. All human beings have the desire for sexual intimacy. It is a yearning for completeness. The magnetic attraction between a man and a woman is innate, powerful, and unyielding.

Of course, we are responsible for what we do with those involuntary sexual feelings. Both the Old Testament and the

New give specific instruction on what sexual activity is permissible and what is not. Like fire, which can either heat a house or burn it down, we are created with powerful natural forces of attraction that must be controlled.

BEARING THE MAKER'S IMAGE

What separates man from the animal world is that he was created in God's image. "Let us make man in our image, in our likeness, and let them rule over the fish of the sea and the birds of the air, over the livestock, over all the earth, and over all the creatures that move along the ground" (Genesis 1:26). Notice that man was not to rule over the woman; but the woman was to be co-ruler under his authority and dominion. Thus, let *them* rule . . .

God gave Adam and Eve different characteristics. Men tend to be aggressive and depend upon a rational analysis of life's problems. Women have a strong sense of intuition, basic trust, and sensitivity. Obviously, these are generalizations and there is overlapping. The point is simply that both genders mirror different aspects of God on earth. Both genders bear the image of God, though they reflect God in different ways.

Then comes the account of their marriage. "For this reason a man will leave his father and mother and be united to his wife, and they will become one flesh. The man and his wife were both naked, and they felt no shame" (Genesis 2:24–25). That word *one* should catch our attention. Marriage brings a unity that is unlike anything else on this earth; indeed, it represents a unity found only in heaven—in *God* Himself!

That Hebrew word *one* is found elsewhere in the Old Testament, specifically in the words, "Hear, O Israel! The LORD is our God, the LORD is One!" (Deuteronomy 6:4). Yes, the same Hebrew word for *one* (*ehad*) is used in the verse quoted above, "and they shall become *one* flesh" (Genesis 2:24). In other words, marriage is to represent the plurality and unity of God in the Trinity. Just as it is unthinkable that members of the Trinity would operate as separate entities, so a husband and wife should operate together with diversity within unity. The bond that has been formed involves the total personality of each partner. To quote the words of theologian Walter Brueggemann, "Humanity in community is male and female. And one is the full image of God alone."[1]

To put it clearly, the original purpose of marriage was to mirror God! Yes, those couples who do not acknowledge the God of the Bible can also find meaning in their marriage relationships. Thanks to "common grace" the spiritual unity of a man and a woman can be accepted and enjoyed even if its origin and purpose is unknown. Indeed, we all have known Christian marriages, which were to say the least, a discredit to the God-ordained plan, many of them ending in a bitter divorce. Thanks to the Fall, we can only dimly recover the divine mandate, but that should not keep us from trying. For only through an understanding of biblical unity can we achieve fulfillment.

Nothing said here should imply that those who are single are any less representative of the image of God. We can represent God in different ways and in a variety of relationships. But it is in the community of male and female that God's image is more fully represented. Later in this book we shall speak of chaste singleness in more detail.

BIND US TOGETHER

In marriage, a man and a woman are joined by two bonds. The first is a *covenant*, an agreement that they will live together until "death does them part." The second is the *sexual relationship* that forms a spiritual bond that has already been referred to and will be explained in more detail later.

It is true the Bible does not mention the wedding ceremony as we know it. But in Old Testament times the bride and groom did enter into an agreement, even if it was not ratified in the same way as we do today. Even in the case of Isaac and Rebekah, a covenant was made between Abraham (Isaac's father) and Laban (Rebekah's father). This agreement was spoken by Abraham's servant (Genesis 24:48–49). Gifts were given to signify the betrothal.

Even cultures that have no roots in Judeo-Christian teaching have various rituals, but the marriage of a man and a woman is almost universally celebrated as a time of social affirmation. As cultures change, so do the customs accompanying the wedding ceremony. What these rituals affirm is the recognition that a man and a woman should not live together without the benefit of a solemn covenantal agreement.

After the covenantal bond comes the sexual bond that unites two people in a spiritual relationship, body, soul and spirit. One person who bears the image of God, figuratively speaking, stamps his or her image on the partner who also bears the image of God. When two bodies unite in intimate sexual relationship, two *souls* are also joined together. Sex forms a "soul tie" with the partner that unites them in a spiritual oneness. To the ancient Jews, sex within marriage was properly considered a holy act. On his wedding night it was said that a man actually went into the Holy of Holies when he made love to his wife.

In his excellent book, *Sacred Sex*, Tim Allan Gardner writes, "Sex was created, inaugurated, and blessed by the source of holiness, God Himself. Before sin entered the world, God gave sex as a divinely unique and extraordinary gift to the original couple to share and enjoy with each other, to celebrate their oneness. Sex is holy as well because it is in sex, in the full unity of both male and female, that the image of God is represented."[2] This explains why Paul taught that marriage should give a concrete display of the relationship between Christ and the church. Sometimes we get the impression that when Paul wanted an illustration of the relationship between husband and wife, it dawned on him that Christ and the Church would be a great parallel. But deeper reflection leads to the conclusion that *the very purpose of marriage was to reflect the relationship between Christ and the church.*

He says that wives should submit to their husbands, "For the husband is the head of the wife as Christ is the head of the Church . . ." To those women who believe such submission is victimization and to husbands who misuse this principle, Paul continues, "Husbands, love your wives, just as Christ loved the church and gave himself up for her to make her holy, cleansing her by the washing of water through the word. . . ." We should not be surprised that he ends this section by quoting Genesis, "For this reason a man will leave his father and mother and will be united to his wife, and the two will become *one* flesh" (Ephesians 5:25, 26, 31).

And so marriage creates two bonds. Sexual intimacy is to be enjoyed under the protection of a covenant of commitment, caring, and unconditional love. Thus two become one flesh.

SEXUAL BONDS WITHOUT A COVENANT

Some Bible scholars teach that since sex bonds two people together, couples who have shared a bed are already married. According to this view, premarital sex does not exist, for sex equals marriage. This teaching has caused young people to get married, even to partners they neither loved nor respected. Their reasoning is clear: If they are already married in the sight of God, they should complete the union by having a formal wedding ceremony.

However, sexual intercourse in and of itself does not constitute marriage. A man and woman are made husband and wife by a covenant taken in the presence of God and witnesses. The Lord rebuked Israelite men for mistreating their wives and said to each one, "She is your partner, the wife of your marriage covenant" (Malachi 2:14). The covenant justifies the sexual relationship; the sexual relationship does not justify the covenant.

Today millions of couples are cohabiting without the benefit of a marriage covenant. In most instances this arrangement serves as a back door of escape, just in case the relationship does not work out. But this arrangement communicates a confusing dual message. On the one hand the partners are saying to each other, "I love you so much I want to be sexually intimate with you." On the other hand the second message is, "I don't want to get too close to you so that I have the option of escaping in case you don't meet all of my needs." According to P. Roger Hillerstrom, "The result of this double message is an inbred lack of confidence in the relationship."[3] Understandably, these seeds of doubt bear bitter fruit later on.

Some ask, "What difference does a piece of paper make?" We answer with another question: "Would you buy a house without signing such a 'piece of paper'?" Of course not. One reason for signing a piece of paper is to prevent one of the parties from backing out when a better deal comes along. To carry the analogy one step further: After the papers are signed, you have the right to move into the new premises and enjoy them. After the marriage covenant, the couple now has the right to enjoy one another in the sexual relationship.

God intended that the first sexual experience be enjoyed by a man and a woman who are wholly committed to each other with the protection of a covenant. That was to assure the acceptance and unconditional love that must guard the most intimate of all human relationships.

Once that bond has been established, it must be nurtured and strengthened with trust and respect. When the commitment is threatened, the sexual fulfillment (at least on the part of one partner, if not both) is diminished. The danger is that sex is reduced to an erotic biological experience divorced from its spiritual meaning.

Most of us were raised with necessary warnings about illicit sexual expression. But if this is all that we know about what God says on the subject, we will live with a sense of shame or at least embarrassment. The prohibitions of Scripture (such as "Thou shalt not commit adultery") are only one side of the coin; we also must understand God's intention in giving us these desires. We must strive to handle our sexuality in such a way that these desires will fulfill us and not destroy us.

Though the sex drive is powerful, no person need think that sex is necessary for either happiness or fulfillment. Many who are single testify to the contentment of their lifestyle. Others who are married may not be able to have sex because of physical disabilities or other mitigating factors. It is not necessary to have sexual intercourse in order to accept our sexuality.

Sexuality and Alien Bonds

Every sexual relationship apart from the man/woman relationship in marriage can be called an *alien* bond; that is, a bond that violates the biblical boundaries. Perhaps one of the most helpful passages in the New Testament regarding the nature of sexuality is found in Paul's words to the Corinthian church. "Do you not know that your bodies are members of Christ himself? Shall I then take the members of Christ and unite them with a prostitute? Never! Do you now know that he who unites himself with a prostitute is one with her in body? For it is said, 'The two will become one flesh'" (1 Corinthians 6:15–16).

Incredibly, Paul says that when a man has sex with a prostitute, that is, sex without a commitment, sex without a hint of mutual respect or caring—in a relationship based on the exploitation of raw lust—even then "the two will become one flesh." Sex binds two people together not just physically, but also in the soul and spirit even apart from marriage.

Sex with a prostitute forms an alien bond, a bond outside the boundaries and nurture of a marriage covenant. This bond is an intruder, a violation of what God intended. Two persons have come together in an intimate union without the security of a covenant based on respect and trust.

A woman whose husband asked her forgiveness for his promiscuity said, "I feel as if all the other women he has had sex with are in bed there with me." In a sense she was right. AIDS researchers tell us that when we have a sexual relationship, we are, in effect, having sex with all the people our partner has had sex with. This is true medically, but it is also true metaphysically. Because sex joins people into one flesh, past "bonds" are still there. Their power can only be removed by forgiveness and the cleansing of the conscience.

When the first sexual experience (or subsequent ones) occurs outside the marriage covenant, the sexual bond can be so powerful that it can even determine the direction of the person's sexual orientation. A boy recruited by an older homosexual may initially hate the experience, but because sex binds two people together, he may begin to feel a sense of security and fulfillment within this relationship. Soon he seeks out other partners, not because he was born a homosexual, but because his initial experiences were so stamped upon his soul that he now follows the lead of his newly awakened desires.

IT IS PRECISELY BECAUSE SEX TOUCHES THE HUMAN SOUL THAT SEXUAL ABUSE IN THE LIFE OF A CHILD CAN BE SO DIFFICULT TO OVERCOME.

This also explains why a young woman may marry a man with whom she has slept even though he may be abusive. His soul is indelibly imprinted on her mind and heart, and she feels an obligation to become his wife. Because of sex, he also may have incredible power over her. He may mistreat her, but she will usually return to him. Even if the relationship ends, she will find it difficult to put him out of her mind. Understandably, the next step is to begin the cycle of promiscuity, hoping to find that elusive meaningful connection, which will finally satisfy.

It is precisely because sex has a spiritual dimension and therefore touches the human soul that sexual abuse in the life of a child can be so difficult, or perhaps even impossible, to overcome. Far from being simply a biological experience that "feels good," it is a gross spiritual ritual which pollutes the conscience and therefore disconnects the soul from God and others. It is the fuel that lights the fires of shame and the frantic desire for other relationships, no matter how broken. In a word, it is the path to addiction.

DESECRATING THE BODY

Same-sex marriages fall outside the boundaries of a one-man, one-woman relationship, and so are alien bonds, intruders that desecrate the body and pollute the soul. When humans try use sex to embrace the spiritual part of themselves and ignore God's design, they always come up short. Of necessity all alien bonds are cut off from God's intentions and thus violate the original marriage charter. The spiritual dimension of the relationship is destroyed.

Although I don't agree with everything M. Scott Peck has written, he perceptively notes in *Further Along the Road Less Traveled*, "Sex is the closest that many people ever come to spiritual experience. Indeed, it is because it is a spiritual experience of sorts that so many chase after it with a repetitive, desperate kind of abandon. Often, whether they know it or not, they are searching for God."[4] Yes, the pursuit of a sexual partner is, for the homosexual or heterosexual, at root a search for God. But sex, separated from God's holy intention, is reduced to a biological experience that falls victim to the law of diminishing returns. Such relationships cannot represent the intimacy between Christ and the church, nor can they represent the real presence of God, but the presence of an alien, impure spirit. *Alien bonds of whatever kind are the antithesis of holiness.*

Individuals, whether homosexual or heterosexual, seldom have an abiding commitment to alien bonds. And because they have experienced intimacy outside the proper boundaries, they will have a tendency to forgo any process of courtship and almost immediately seek genital intimacy. Now that the principle of a covenant relationship of one man and one woman has been violated, the temptation to continue the spiral will be persistent and powerful.

To affirm same-sex marriages is to take one more step to cut sex off from its God blessed intention of mirroring plurality and unity. In short, to affirm same-sex marriages is to toss aside the Owner's Manual, intent on finding our own way, at any cost. With it we add more brokenness to our brave new world of social experimentation.

The Bible gives several purposes for sex. One is to mirror unity in diversity; another is pleasure. But high on the list is that children might be born into an environment where they can grow and flourish as men and women. God intended that as a result of the loving union of the one-man, one-woman relationship, children would be born into an atmosphere of security, where both genders model teamwork and commitment.

It is to the children we now turn.

We Must Remember the Children

3

People drift along from generation to generation, and the morally unthinkable becomes thinkable as the years move on.

—FRANCIS SCHAEFFER

MANY OF US, when considering the possibility of a homosexual couple parenting children, feel a profound unease—but we cannot exactly say why. It simply feels . . . wrong. Even beyond the biblical proscriptions, such arrangements strike us as violating something deeply rooted in our very biology. They're unnatural.

Survey the cultures of the world and you will discover that the concept of "family" is found in all of them. Certain tribes practice bigamy or even polygamy, but they all have the sense that children belong to the parents who gave them birth. There is a connectedness between men and women, and the result is offspring for whom they care.

Despite the radical differences among cultures, they all have a moral consciousness and a commitment to their family, an "internal guidance system." Since every part of us is tainted

THE MORAL CONSCIOUSNESS FOUND THROUGHOUT THE WORLD CAN ONLY BE EXPLAINED BY "COMMON GRACE" GIVEN TO ALL PEOPLE, BASED ON NATURAL LAW.

with sin, our consciences are not always reliable and we can also turn a deaf ear to what we know is right. Yet we are all born with a moral compass that lets us know that we are obligated to one another and answerable to a higher power. Through both the conscience and creation, humankind knows that there is a superior moral law.

Obviously, this moral law is often seen imperfectly, and even what is seen is often set aside for personal self-interest. We have all known better than we have lived. But the moral consciousness found throughout the world can only be explained by "common grace" given to all people, based on natural law. Marriage and family are a part of that internal consciousness.

So in many cultures that are not Christian—Japan, for example—marriage is defined as a committed relationship between one man and one woman. The fact that partners may not always be faithful to their vows does not change that. Even in primitive cultures this stands as the ideal. Historically, in no culture of which I am aware—excluding the present social experiments of modern-day Europe—have two lesbians or two homosexual men who are rearing children comprised a "family."

Words can be defined differently, but historically the word *family* has been always understood as "a basic unit in society having as its nucleus a man and a woman who care for their child or children." Though we might speak of a "single-parent family," this very qualification reminds us that in such an arrangement the family might still be said to exist, but it is fractured, either because of divorce or death.

Though some homosexual radicals disdain the concept of natural law, such laws have been recognized in all cultures and among all the different religions of the world. Understandably so, for the very anatomy of a man and a woman tells us that these two genders were meant for one another.

According to the gay newspaper the *Windy City Times*, a Cleveland City Council hopeful could not be appointed to the council because when asked whether he supported same-sex marriages, he replied that he considered marriage to be a matter of "natural law." That was enough to bar Patrick Corrigan from his appointment.[1]

Paul, when speaking about homosexuals, writes, "Even their women exchanged natural relations with unnatural ones. In the same way the men also abandoned natural relations with women and were inflamed with lust for one another" (Romans 1:26, 27). Thus a homosexual is actually fighting against his own nature. Evidence suggests that the reason there are more teen suicides among homosexuals is not because of the ridicule they receive from heterosexuals, but rather because of the inner conflict that the lifestyle of necessity brings with it.[2]

Marriage between one woman and one man is rooted in the natural creation. Princeton University sociologist Sara McLanahan wrote:

> If we were asked to design a system for making sure that children's basic needs were met, we would probably come up with something quite similar to the two-parent

ideal. Such a design, in theory, would not only ensure that children had access to the time and money of two adults, it would also provide a system of checks and balances that promoted quality parenting. The fact that both parents have a biological connection to the child would increase the likelihood that the parents would identify with the child and be willing to sacrifice for that child, and it would reduce the likelihood that either parent would abuse the child.[3]

Much as some might hate the Designer, they cannot deny the fact that we are born with the Designer's label. God established a pattern and we do well to follow it.

THE ADOPTION QUESTION

WE CANNOT WREST CHILDREN FROM THE GOD-GIVEN FORMAT OF FAMILY RELATIONSHIPS WITHOUT SERIOUS CONSEQUENCES.

When Rosie O'Donnell adopted a child, the youngster was not the product of the relationship between two lesbians, or for that matter, between two gay men. No, that child was the product of a man and a woman. If we are planning to redefine the concept of *family*, we must ask what being raised by gay couples will mean for children.

We can already hear a chorus of objections, "But think of the abuse there is in some traditional man-woman marriages! Isn't it better to have a child raised by two loving, caring lesbians, or two or more loving, caring homosexual men?"

Yes, of course it would be better for a child to be raised by two loving lesbians than an abusive heterosexual couple. The issue is not whether two lesbians can love a child and take care of its needs. However, our preference should always be to the family in which there is one father and one mother. We cannot wrest children from the God-given format of family relationships without serious consequences. What homosexual adoption fails to take into account are the implications within the wider culture if such relationships were to become commonplace. We would expect—and the research bears this out—that a child reared in the *Heather Has Two Mommies* atmosphere of today's world will suffer from gender confusion or worse.

Of course the gay community is quick to say that there are "no adverse effects" if a child would be reared by two mommies or two daddies. But keep in mind that the research in this area is often done by those who are proponents of such arrangements. Sociologist Steven Nock of the University of Virginia, who is "agnostic" on same-sex marriage, said as an expert witness in a Canadian court that was considering same-sex marriages, "Through this analysis I draw my conclusions that 1) all the articles I reviewed contained at least one fatal flaw of design nor execution; and 2) not a single one of those studies was conducted according general accepted standards of scientific research."[4]

It is worth pointing out that even though evidence on child outcomes is sketchy, Judith Stacey, a sociologist and an advocate for same-sex marriage, agrees that sons of lesbians are less masculine and daughters of lesbians are more masculine. She also found that a "significantly greater proportion of young adult children raised by lesbian mothers than those raised by heterosexual mothers" report homoerotic attractions.[5] It is foolish to think that alternate forms of the family are as good as the father and mother who raise their children together.

PERILS TO PARENTHOOD?

Mary Stewart van Leeuwen, a Christian feminist, says, "It may well be that, irony of ironies, in promoting gay households we may be promoting misogyny . . . People who are gay-positive tend to think that whatever is good for gays is automatically good for people who care about justice for women." She acknowledges that the "gender injustice" of fatherlessness is already a problem in today's society without gay marriage, but added, "I don't think we should add to the possibility of more of it."[6] She predicts unforeseen consequences from such a radical overhaul of marriage and family.

Gay marriage might well change society's entire concept of parenthood. Because gay couples cannot produce children on their own, James Skillen of the Center for Public Justice predicts that hopeful parents may seek to rent wombs and deny children to know their biological parents. "It is going to be increasingly possible to produce, buy, and sell children, because in addition to adoption, that is the only way homosexual couples can 'have' children."[7] Whether raised by lesbians or two homosexual men, *these children will be denied either a mother or a father*.

We all know that a daughter raised in a strong marriage will know what to look for in a man and be better able to resist those who want to take advantage of her sexually. Lesbian mothers are saying that a father is irrelevant to parenting; homosexual fathers say that a mother is irrelevant to parenting. But God says both a mother and a father are relevant to parenting. Is anyone serious in suggesting that two men can take the place of a mother's love, or two women can equal a dad?

God intended that every child have a mother and a father who are an example of commitment, caring, and love. Not only is such a child given a sense of security, but he or she also sees femininity and masculinity modeled in a complementary relationship. Of course in our world with rampant divorce, immorality, and the redefinition of the family, this ideal is becoming a memory. However—and this is important—we must work toward the ideal even though we know we shall not achieve it, rather than work against it, defying the Designer who made us all.

WHEN WE NEED A VILLAGE

When Hillary Clinton wrote her book *It Takes a Village*, some who take issue with her political point of view responded with "No, Hillary . . . it takes a *family*!" They were right, of course; it does take a family—but what happens when there is no family?

If you've not read Hillary's book, you might be surprised to find that it has much in it with which we can agree, like this paragraph:

> In addition, however [to adults needing to know the needs of a child], every society requires a critical mass of families that fit the traditional ideal, both to meet the needs of most children and to serve as a model for other adults who are raising children in difficult settings. We are at risk of losing that critical mass in America today. Parenting has never been easy, but today, when most adults consciously choose to become mothers and

fathers, we owe an even higher degree of love and respect to the children we bring into the world.[8]

Yes, we are in danger of losing that "critical mass." This is an opportunity for the church to be the church. An excellent example of how Christians can become involved in the lives of children from broken homes comes to us from Calvary Chapel in Ft. Lauderdale, Florida. Pastor Bob Coy has challenged the couples in his congregation to be willing to adopt children, or at least become involved in foster care. The church has taken this challenge so seriously that they even provide training for foster parents and assist in the steps of the adoption process.

Also, a meeting was held with over sixty churches and faith-based organizations to discuss the challenge of adoption and foster care. As a result, many couples in Calvary Church and in other churches in the area are now adoptive and foster parents. Hundreds of children now have loving parents to take care of them. Unless we are willing to model such commitment, we are in no position to be critical of homosexual adoptions.

The church must step up to the plate at this critical hour!

An Unlikely Ally

If someone would have told me just a year ago that I would be recommending a book by a pro-abortion, lesbian feminist, I would not have believed it. Yet incredibly, Tammy Bruce, in *The Death of Right and Wrong*, has written a book that exposes the agenda of the radical left as none other that I've read.

In the mid-1990s, Tammy Bruce was the president of the Los Angeles chapter of the National Organization of Women. As such she was able to witness firsthand the left's attempts to undermine our millennia-old code of morals and values. She watched as the leadership of NOW drifted from its original purpose of fighting for women's rights and degenerated into an organization that sought to undercut all distinctions between right and wrong in order to foist their own amoral

HOW BETTER TO TRULY BELONG TO THE MAJORITY (WHEN YOU'RE REALLY ON THE FRINGE) THAN BY TAKING POSSESSION OF THE NEXT GENERATION?

agenda on the country. In this crusade it was joined by other groups with the intent of reordering society as we know it. These groups, she says, have the intention of *bending society to mirror their warped view of the world.*

She points out that for the radicals, it is not a matter of accepting homosexuality but rather it has "everything to do with eliminating the lines of decency and morality across the board. Instead of being about tolerance and equal treatment under the law, today's gay movement, in the hands of extremists, now uses the language of rights to demand acceptance of the depraved, the damaged and the malignantly narcissistic."[9]

Since this chapter is on children, I shall quote one of her passages at length. It deserves a careful read:

> Today's gay activists have carried the campaign a step further, invading children's lives by wrapping themselves in the banner of tolerance. It is literally the

equivalent of the wolf coming to your door dressed as your grandmother.

The radicals in control of the gay establishment want children in their world of moral decay, lack of self-restraint, and moral relativism. Why? How better to truly belong to the majority (when you're really on the fringe) than by taking possession of the next generation? By targeting children, you can start indoctrinating the next generation with the false construct that gay people deserve special treatment and special laws. How else can the gay establishment actually get society to believe, borrowing from George Orwell, that gay people are indeed more equal than others? Of course, the only way to get that idea accepted is to condition people into accepting nihilism that forbids morality and judgment.[10]

Bruce devotes an entire chapter to a book by Judith Levine titled *Harmful to Minors: The Perils of Protecting Children From Sex*. We might dismiss this book, which advocates sex with children, as an aberration, the work of a disengaged activist who speaks for no one but herself. Sadly, this is not so. Levine is respected in many circles and is highly regarded in academia.

Tammy Bruce believes the reason these ideas are widely accepted is that "sexualizing children," as she calls it, guarantees control of the culture for future generations. She writes, "It also promises sex-addicted future consumers on which the porn industry relies. By destroying those lives, they strike the final blow to family, faith, tradition, decency, and judgment."[11]

Certainly the majority of homosexuals would, I'm sure, disagree with Levine's book—as I've noted, we must be careful not to paint all of them with a broad brush. But we must be aware that lying at the core of the radical homosexual movement is the desire to "sexualize children" for the purpose of control and conditioning. There is no question that same-sex marriages would be another step down this perilous path.

Francis Schaeffer, who helped awaken the evangelical church to its cultural responsibilities back in the 1970s, would not be surprised were he to step into our world today. He presciently wrote:

> There is a "thinkable" and an "unthinkable" in every era. One era is quite certain intellectually and emotionally about what is acceptable. Yet another era decides that these "certainties" are unacceptable and puts another set of values into practice. On a humanistic base, people drift along from generation to generation, and the morally unthinkable becomes thinkable as the years move on.[12]

Writing in the 1970s, he went on to say that the "thinkables" of the '80s and '90s will certainly include things which most people today find unthinkable and even immoral, even unimaginable and too extreme to suggest. He concludes with this clincher, "Yet—since they do not have some overriding principle that takes them beyond relativistic thinking—when these become thinkable and acceptable . . . most people will not even remember that they were unthinkable in the seventies. *They will slide into each new thinkable without a jolt.*"[13]

Unless we return to God in repentance, we can expect the unthinkable to become thinkable before our eyes. Indeed, it already has.

THE FAMILY AND GOD'S JUDGMENT

"Who are we hurting?" asked Barney Frank, an openly gay congressman from Massachusetts, about homosexuals' desire to marry.[14] Many Americans, including, perhaps, some who worship with us on Sunday, wonder the same thing: How does redefining marriage and family affect our own marriages, our own families?

But we are learning that two incompatible understandings of the family cannot exist side by side for very long. This is why those who advocate same-sex marriages are adamant that the traditional concept of family must be reordered—if not destroyed.

The family, however, was to be God's means of propagating the truth of His Word from one generation to another. Fathers were to teach their sons and daughters the law of the Lord. "These commandments that I give you today are to be upon your hearts. Impress them on your children. Talk about them when you sit at home and when you walk along the road, when you lie down and when you get up. Tie them as symbols on your hands and bind them on your foreheads. Write them on the doorframes of your houses and on your gates" (Deuteronomy 6:6–9).

The connection between fathers and their sons, mothers and their daughters—in short, the concept of the biblical family—lies at the heart of Judaism and Christianity. The family is to be guarded, valued, and protected. When we speak of the "sanctity of marriage" this is not just a pious phrase; it is the essence of life, the environment in which values are formed, and future generations are guided.

What happens when a nation turns from God and seeks its own way? In the case of Israel, God would allow the nation to be overrun by enemies. In the book of Judges we read repeatedly that God told the nation something like this, "Because this nation has violated the covenant that I laid down for their forefathers and has not listened to me, I will no longer drive out before them any of the nations Joshua left when he died. I

WHEN WE TURN FROM THE LORD, HE DOES NOT FIGHT FOR US, BUT ALLOWS US TO BE DISTRESSED BY THOSE WHO OPPOSE US.

will use them to test Israel and see whether they will keep the way of the LORD and walk in it as their forefathers did" (2:20). Thus, God "sold" them into the hands of other nations.

But God's final judgment was not political slavery, severe though that was. When the nation failed to learn its lessons, God allowed the coming of invaders to destroy the nation's families. The slavery of children, the loneliness and pain of being torn from mother and father, the distress of parents— all were God's judgment for squandered opportunities.

Listen to what God has to say to a nation that has turned from Him. "Your sons and daughters will be given to another nation, and you will wear out your eyes watching for them day after day, powerless to lift a hand. . . . You will have sons and daughters but you will not keep them because they will go into captivity . . . Because you did not serve the LORD your God joyfully and gladly in the time of prosperity, therefore in hunger and thirst, in nakedness and dire poverty, you will serve the enemies the LORD sends against you. He will put an iron yoke on your neck until he has destroyed you" (Deuteronomy 28:32, 41, 47, 48). And so it was that God brought other nations to Israel and He refused to fight in their behalf.

Of course our judgment will look quite different than the picture described by Moses 3,500 years ago. But the principle remains: When we turn from the Lord, He does not fight for us, but allows us to be distressed by those who oppose us. The result is ruptured relationships, children suffering, growing up without their parents, and the inability to do anything about it.

As the *Family Research Report* says, "Every time the mortar that holds society together is weakened, another step toward the destruction of society is made. Marriage is one of the most important elements in our societal mortar; and thus we can expect it to be attacked by all those who hate our society or its Christian heritage."[15]

We have blithely tolerated divorce; we have allowed the media to steal the hearts of our children; we have followed materialism and pleasure. In these and a dozen other ways we have drunk greedily from the fountains of the world. Now we are beginning to reap the whirlwind. Yes, God is there for us, but only if we humble ourselves and repent in this critical hour. If not, the fate of Israel's families might be that of our own.

We Must Resist the Pressure

4

One can . . . love [gay couples] as fellow family members or just as fellow human beings, and still fight for the preservation of marriage as every civilization has known it.

—DENNIS PRAGER

TWO LESBIANS, both from Christian families, said that their relationship was not only loving but "beautiful." In fact, they were more certain that their relationship with one another was honoring to God than they were about anything else. Since God created them with a different "orientation," why would the Almighty not be pleased with how they expressed their love to one another? If heterosexuals could enjoy the bliss of wedded love, why would a good God deprive them of the same privilege?

The pressure to affirm same-sex marriages is relentless. We hear it from the media, from some politicians and from the gays themselves who plead with us to see their point: They also are human beings with sexual desires; it would be unfair for some people to express those desires while others are forbidden to do so. And what human being—family member or otherwise—has the right to deny them equal status in matters of vocation and marriage?

When we hear these arguments long enough, as we saw earlier, they can wear us down like the continuous dripping of water on stone. Eventually we begin to think, *Well, maybe* . . .

That's exactly what gay activists hope we'll think.

In this chapter we will consider many of the specific arguments in favor of homosexual relationships and, therefore, same-sex marriage. We will explore how some of today's leading research invalidates those arguments. And, in the process, we will, I hope, provide God's people a way to resist the relentless drip-drip and in response lovingly, truthfully, and convincingly speak.

In their very insightful book *Homosexuality: The Use of Scientific Research in the Church's Moral Debate*, psychologists Stanton L. Jones and Mark A. Yarhouse interact with both moral theology and contemporary science, reviewing many of the arguments put forward by the gay community and showing them to be flawed. In many of the instances below I draw on their research.

"I Was Born That Way"

The oft-stated argument goes like this: If it can be established that homosexuality is caused genetically rather than a chosen lifestyle, then homosexuality cannot be immoral.[1] And so there is the search for the so-called "gay gene" with the hope that it can be proven that homosexuality, like skin color, is not freely chosen. Thus, in the minds of the public it follows with impeccable logic that gays are not responsible for their gayness, thus are free to act on their feelings. As one homosexual advocate put it, "Only a sadistic God would create hundreds of thousands of humans to be inherently homosexual and then deny them the right to sexual intimacy."[2] In brief, since gayness is created by God, the homosexual lifestyle must be affirmed.

This obviously is not the place to evaluate the evidence on whether homosexuality is genetic, although so far virtually all studies that insist it is genetic suffer from glaring methodological flaws.[3] My concern has only to do with the logic behind the "If it is genetic . . . then it must be affirmed" equation. Even if homosexuality is shown to be genetic—and so far the evidence is far from conclusive—this would not yield the results that are so blithely assumed.

EVEN IF WE ARGUE THAT WE ARE BORN WITH CERTAIN PREDISPOSITIONS, WE STILL HAVE HUMAN RESPONSIBILITY FOR OUR LIFESTYLES AND ACTIONS.

First, we must better understand the nature of genetics itself. There is a difference between those genes that make up the body and those genes that influence our desires and predispositions. Jones and Yarhouse write, "We are used to thinking of genes as causing us to have things like brown eyes or wavy hair, and choice has little to do with such characteristics. But behavioral genetics has produced abundant evidence of genetic influences that clearly do not render human choice irrelevant."[4]

We are responsible for our behavior *even if it is genetically motivated*. Surely homosexuals don't want to say that their genes have rendered them helpless robots, incapable of human choice about their behavior.[5] They would want to affirm, I think, that they are moral agents who should be held accountable for their lifestyle. In other words, no matter what influence our genetic makeup has on us, we cannot use this as an excuse for a lack of accountability and responsibility.

Many years ago I met a kleptomaniac who tried to steal practically anything he saw. He even stole merchandise when there was every reason to believe he would be caught. Though he was punished for shoplifting, he continued his lifestyle, saying that the "buzz" he received from trying to get past the checkout counter motivated him to repeat his behavior. "I've always wanted to steal as far back as I can remember," he said. Then he added, "There's no question in my mind that it's genetic."

So what do we do if we find a kleptomaniac gene, a pedophile gene, or an alcoholic gene? Even if we argue that we are born with certain predispositions, we still have human responsibility for our lifestyles and actions. Ever since the Fall in Eden, we all have a predisposition to sin. These fallen desires (often referred to as *lusts* in Scripture) must be channeled, directed, and often denied the fulfillment they crave.

When we hear someone say that he or she has a "right" to homosexual behavior, we have to point out that sexual intimacy is not a right. Rather than the language of rights, we have to return to the language of obligations. And in the Bible, it is clear that we have an obligation to be sexually chaste if we are not married and sexually faithful if we are. We cannot argue that our desires are "from God" and therefore worthy of fulfillment.

C. S. Lewis, with searing logic, wrote, "From the statement of psychological fact, 'I have an impulse to do so and so' we cannot by any ingenuity derive the practical principle, 'I ought to obey this impulse . . .' Telling us to obey instinct is like telling us to obey 'people.' People say different things: so do instincts. Our instincts are at war."[6]

Regardless of our sexual desires, whether genetic or acquired, we are creatures created with the ability to choose, and we are held accountable to God for those choices. We cannot argue that the devil or our genes "made us do it."

"HOMOSEXUALITY CANNOT BE CHANGED"

This, perhaps, is the crux of the debate—for if homosexuals *cannot* change, so the argument goes, then it would be the worst sort of coldheartedness to deny them the happiness and fulfillment that the rest of us enjoy. And again, more and more good church people are listening and wondering. . . .

So *can* homosexuals change?

There is plenty of evidence to suggest that the answer is yes, given the thousands of former homosexuals who give testimony that they have been changed. Organizations such as Exodus International have for years shared real-life testimonies of those who have left the lifestyle and have even had their desires transformed, and are now living in heterosexual marriage.

Many gays, however, routinely dismiss these accounts out of hand, saying that such people were never "truly" homosexual—bolstering their argument that change is both impossible and undesirable. Even the very idea that one would want to change is seen as a denial of one's fundamental personhood. Thus the chasm between those who claim deliverance and those who insist such claims are spurious.

My purpose is not to evaluate the evidence, but rather to ask this question: even if someone finds that he or she cannot change to heterosexual desires, does this justify living the homosexual lifestyle? Anyone acquainted with the New Testament has read Paul's words,

> *Do you not know that the wicked will not inherit the kingdom of God? Do not be deceived: Neither the sexually immoral nor idolaters nor adulterers nor male prostitutes nor homosexual offenders nor thieves nor the greedy nor drunkards nor slanderers nor swindlers will inherit the kingdom of God. And that is what some of you were. But you were washed, you were sanctified, you were justified in the name of the Lord Jesus Christ and by the Spirit of our God* (1 CORINTHIANS 6:9–11).

Several important points must be made about this passage: First, that all the sexual sins that we have in our culture were rampant in ancient Corinth; also present were the contemporary sins of slander, thievery, and greed. Second, we learn that the Gospel changed these people. A gospel that does not change the basic aspirations of the human heart is no gospel at all.

However, is Paul saying that homosexuals can be changed into heterosexuals? He does not say that Christ took these people who lived the homosexual lifestyle and transformed their sexual desires so that now they could be happily married. He simply says, "And that is what some of you *were*." And now, they are washed, sanctified, and justified. What Paul might have meant was that these homosexuals now lived their lives in the power of the Holy Spirit and were committed to a life of chastity.[7]

In the same letter, Paul discusses marriage, but also singleness, which he holds in high regard. He discusses various situations in which people find themselves, arguing that the married should stay married, but the singles should be free to stay single. At the end of a rather lengthy discussion, he concludes, "So then he who marries the virgin does right, but he who does not marry her does even better" (7:38). Paul himself, it is believed, never married. He did not deem single-ness as a lifestyle to which one is condemned, but rather a unique opportunity to serve the Lord.

As all of us know, there are many heterosexuals who are denied marriage, either because they have not been able to connect with an ideal suitor, or because they are committed to other interests. There is nothing in the Bible about marriage being a "right" that people can demand. We are not asking more of single homosexuals than we ask of single hetero-sexuals when we insist on chastity.

Jones and Yarhouse write, "It may be that the church can no more guarantee healing to homosexuals than it can guar-antee marriage to disconsolate single heterosexuals. There are many more single Christian heterosexuals 'doomed' to sexual abstinence by the church's 'narrow' sexual morality than there are homosexual persons similarly constrained."[8]

In other words, it would be eminently possible, as many testify, to be committed to chastity even while struggling with homosexual desires, just as heterosexuals can be committed to chastity while struggling with their desires. Paul says that the interests of married people are divided, but that those who are single can live with "undivided devotion to the Lord" (v. 35).

Chaste homosexuals (ex-gays), like chaste heterosexuals, must be enfolded within the community of the church. They need the support of the wider Christian community, and the larger family of God. Singles, I've learned, can serve the Lord in many ways that we as married people cannot. In the next chapter we shall expand on this.

"GAY MARRIAGE IS A MATTER OF CIVIL RIGHTS"

Some gay activists have attempted to equate their drive for legal marriage with the great battles for civil rights fought by black Americans over the past century—a strategy that has met with mixed response in the black community itself. Dwight A. McBride, writing in the *Chicago Tribune*, is a gay African-American man who supports such efforts and criticizes the Reverend Jesse Jackson for trying to unhitch the link between civil rights and homosexual marriage.

McBride asserts that if we pass a constitutional amendment abridging the right to civil marriage among that class of citizens known as gays and lesbians, we "will be writing into the Constitution an amendment that denies the right of civil marriage for one group of citizens while reserving that right for others."[9] He goes on to say that he is arguing for recognition of civil marriage, not religious practice. Churches can refuse to marry gays, but they "do not have the right to dictate to the government their religious beliefs about who has access to civil marriage."

First, all of us realize that the color of one's skin is not a matter of our choice; that is genetically determined. But as we have already seen, homosexual behavior is not genetically determined, even if scientists were able to locate the elusive "gay gene." It is one thing to say that we believe in civil rights for all regardless of one's skin color. It is quite another to say that we believe in civil rights for all regardless of one's behavior.

Second, this leads to the question of personhood itself. Homosexuals frequently speak of themselves as if their gayness is fundamental to who they are as persons—that they are in effect defined by their gayness. As a result they set themselves off as a separate class, a group that needs special attention and deference.

There is no question that our identity is to a great extent bound up with our gender: Male and female He created them. Part of that identity is the fact that we have sexual desires. However, to essentially affirm, "I am my desires" is to give our sexual passions a wrongful place on the scale of values. Jones and Yarhouse state it well: We must not forget that "much that is fundamental to our identities is bad—we are, after all, sinful and fallen to the core and while that is part of our identities, it is not something around which to cultivate an identity."[10]

MANY WHO HAVE COME OUT OF THE GAY LIFESTYLE SAY THAT THEIR JOURNEY BEGAN WHEN THEY NO LONGER THOUGHT OF GAYNESS AS THE ESSENCE OF THEIR PERSONHOOD.

Personhood is more than my particular sexual passions. Gays, like the rest of us, are born either male or female, but they express their masculinity and their femininity in a way that is inconsistent with their original creation. Personhood is essentially who I am created in the image of God; it is the value I have by virtue of my creation and my ability to choose, to love, and to communicate. Most of all, my identity is bound up with my ability to know God as He has revealed Himself in nature and in the Scriptures.

We agree with Jesse Jackson, and a growing number of black ministers, that we must unhitch the supposed connection between civil rights and homosexual rights. After all, no black person has ever abandoned his "blackness," but plenty of people have abandoned their sexual behavior. Many who have come out of the gay lifestyle say that their journey began when they no longer thought of themselves as fundamentally gay, as if gayness was the essence of their personhood.

What about McBride's argument that the church has no right to "dictate" its beliefs to the government? That argument denies the church its rightful role as a contributor to and shaper of culture and as a moral compass to society. The church has every right to inform and influence laws and governmental policies—as do business, education, media, and various other bodies that seek a place in the public square.

Also, we must ask: "Who is dictating what to whom?" The homosexual movement, with its stringent insistence that all opposition be silenced, has been "imposing" its agenda on society with a vengeance.

"JESUS DIDN'T MENTION HOMOSEXUALITY"

The argument here is that since Jesus did not mention homosexuality, evidently He did not think it was wrong. More to the point, He would have emphasized love between human beings at all times, no matter where it was found and no matter the kind of relationship.

First, Jesus upheld the Old Testament and obviously would not have disagreed with its teachings about such moral behavior. Yes, there is a difference between the Old Testament ceremonial regulations, which applied to Israel, and the New Testament, which has instructions for the church. But in moral matters, there is continuity of expression; if anything, the New Testament challenges us to a higher standard of conduct. We do not believe that Jesus' words have more authority than those of the apostle Paul who wrote the book of Romans.

Second, it is unthinkable that Jesus, who said, "But I tell you that anyone who looks at a woman lustfully has already committed adultery with her in his heart" (Matthew 5:28)—it is unthinkable that this same Jesus would approve of the sexual sin that is so strongly condemned in the Old Testament.

ANYONE WHO TAKES THE BIBLE SERIOUSLY KNOWS THAT IT IS OFTEN INTOLERANT AND DISCRIMINATORY.

Third, in point of fact, Jesus did indirectly comment on homosexuality; when asked about divorce, He took his disciples back to Genesis 2: "For this reason a man will leave his father and mother and be united to his wife, and the two will become one flesh" (Matthew 19:5). Thus He returns us to the Creator and emphasizes His original intention and design.

"HOW CAN YOU DISCRIMINATE AGAINST ME?"

The words *intolerance* or *discrimination* are powerful words in our society, used to squash any opinions about moral behavior.

In fact, not only should we keep our opinions to ourselves as to what people do, but we should affirm their lifestyles, no matter how destructive or bizarre. Dennis Prager comments on America's unthinking acceptance of "tolerance":

> When the average American hears the word "intolerance" he jumps through hoops to avoid being associated with such an awful thing. Moreover, it takes a great deal of thought to understand why tolerance has nothing to do with whether we should change the definition of marriage and the family. One can tolerate gay couples, move next door to them, invite them over for a barbecue, love them as fellow family members or just as fellow human beings, and still fight for the preservation of marriage as every civilization has known it.[11]

Anyone who takes the Bible seriously knows that it is often intolerant and discriminatory. It is intolerant of sexual sins among heterosexuals and homosexuals; it loudly discriminates against those who do a variety of evils and those who believe false doctrine. It especially discriminates against those who refuse to accept Jesus as Savior and teaches that they shall be in hell forever.

Our character can be judged by what we tolerate and what we don't tolerate; discrimination lies at the heart of making wise decisions. It is not "discrimination" to say that an applicant must meet some minimal requirement to have a certain status. In the case of marriage that requirement is to marry someone of the opposite sex.

To those who say, "God regards all human beings to be of great worth," we reply, "Yes, that might be, but when you study history, I think you'll agree that at least more than a few human beings who are of great worth have done some very terrible things."

"I'm a Christian and God Accepts My Homosexuality"

We've all heard about the struggles in the more liberal denominations over homosexuality and whether openly gay pastors may serve churches. The pro-gay contingents in these debates throw around words like *inclusive* and *affirming*, painting God's church as a sort of big tent where all may show up—no matter what their behavior. Some gay Christians claim they can be in an active homosexual relationship with God's approval.

True? No. Those who say that they can be in a homosexual relationship with God's approval deceive themselves. They forget that God's desire for us is *costly discipleship* that finds fulfillment whether or not we are involved in an intimate sexual relationship. This message is lost in the "Christian gay-affirming literature."

Read every word of this profound insight from Stanton L. Jones who tells us what is missing in the "Christian and Gay" movement:

> Absent are passionate calls to righteousness and to obedience to God's revealed will. Gone is the New Testament repugnance for sexual immorality and an alternative passion for purity. Gone is the vision for the chaste life of singleness as a lifestyle of dignity and delight. Gone is any sense of how our sexuality, and indeed our faith, can serve purposes beyond meeting

our own needs. Absent is a vision for how our sexuality must be harnessed and channeled to serve higher ends. Absent is a cautious awareness of just how contaminated our lives are by the fall and by sin, and of how profound is our capacity for self-deception and desperate need for God's guidance in how to live our lives. Missing is any deep awareness, to paraphrase G.K. Chesterton, that no restriction God might place on how we should experience our sexuality is as incredible as the raw awareness of what a miraculous gift our sexuality is.[12]

God gives all of us a higher calling. For singles it is one calling, for married people another. But all true believers will pursue the high moral ground. We must be committed to holiness no matter how imperfectly attained. Sexual sin cannot be a part of that commitment.

"Look at the Divorce Rate!"

Here we return to the remarks of Mayor Daley of Chicago, when he said he would "have no problem" if homosexual marriages took place in his city. He added, "Don't talk to me about marriage . . . look at how many divorces there are." I've heard evangelical Christians say essentially the same: "Who are we to talk with all the divorces among us? Why should we deny gays marriage? After all, we aren't doing that great."

So, given the high divorce rate, should we give homosexuals an opportunity where we have failed?

Any thought that homosexual couples will give children a more stable environment is quickly contradicted by the facts. Although lesbians have shown the ability to form long-term relationships, male heterosexuals have a notorious track record for a multitude of sexual partners. A large survey of gay men taken in San Francisco during the height of the gay movement of the pre-AIDS '70s showed that only 10 percent of the respondents could be classified as existing in "close-coupled" relationships, and these relationships could only be characterized as "relatively monogamous" or "relatively less promiscuous." Only 17 percent reported having less than fifty sexual partners.

We might think that the situation has changed since then, but a more recent study of 156 stable, committed male homosexual relationships revealed that none of the more than 100 couples that had been together for more than five years had been

MANY HOMOSEXUAL MALES DISTINGUISH BETWEEN EMOTIONAL FIDELITY AND SEXUAL EXCLUSIVITY.

sexually monogamous or exclusive. The authors of this report, themselves a gay couple, argued that for male couples, sexual monogamy is a passing stage of "internalized homophobia," and that many homosexual males distinguish between emotional fidelity and sexual exclusivity. Emotional and not physical faithfulness matters.[13] In other words, they are free to have other sexual partners as long as they are not emotionally attached to them.

The Handbook of Family Diversity reported a study in which many self-described monogamous couples reported an average of three to five partners in the past year.[14] One study showed that most homosexual men understood sexual relations outside the relationship to be the norm and viewed adopting a monogamous standard as an act of oppression.

While the rate of fidelity within married couples is far from ideal, several studies report that an average of 82 percent of spouses claim to have remained faithful to their commitment.[15] Yes, to our shame, many heterosexual marriages have failed. We as a church have stood by watching families torn asunder. And yet, there is no reason to believe that homosexual couples will give our children a more stable environment.

CONCLUSION

We began this chapter with the comments of two lesbians who insisted that they knew that God wanted them to be together. Parents of such children must listen to their reasoning and their heartfelt pleas to be heard. Compassion, communication, and care must always be exercised in these situations. A judgmental, uncaring attitude has driven count-less people deeper into homosexual patterns and behavior. Few groups in society have faced as much condemnation from the church as homosexuals. We all know that Christ came into the world to save sinners, but often the impression is given that homosexuals are excluded from His love and grace. Such a gospel is unworthy of the name!

Yet we must confess that nowhere are we so willingly deceived as in the matter of sexuality, regardless of whether we are homosexual or heterosexual. I think of the men I've known who have convinced themselves that they should leave their wives and be with another woman because they had met their "soul mate." The Bible and plain reason are set aside in the selfish interests of the relationship of the moment. Then they appeal to God's love to sanctify a sinful relationship.

The problem in our culture is that we begin with our experience and use it as a basis to interpret reality. We think, "I'm having this experience and enjoying it, so God in particular and society as a whole had better get used to it and fit in around with what I'm doing." When Paul speaks of God's displeasure regarding sexual sin, he often uses the word *deceived*, or something to that effect, because he knows that the human mind is capable of rationalizing anything the human heart wants to do. Nowhere is this longing to be deceived more pronounced than when justifying an immoral relationship. I've taken the liberty to emphasize words or phrases so Paul's warnings can be more clearly seen.

> **Do not be deceived:** *God cannot be mocked. A man reaps what he sows. The one who sows to please his sinful nature, from that nature will reap destruction; the one who sows to please the Spirit, from the Spirit will reap eternal life."* (GALATIANS 6:7, 8)

> **For of this you can be sure:** *No immoral, impure or greedy person—such a man is an idolater—has any inheritance in the kingdom of Christ and God.* Let no one deceive you with empty words, *for because of such things God's wrath comes on those who are disobedient. Therefore do not be partners with them.* (EPHESIANS 5:5–7)

> **Do not be deceived:** *Neither the sexually immoral nor idolaters nor adulterers nor male prostitutes nor homosexual offenders nor thieves nor the greedy nor drunkards nor slanderers nor swindlers will inherit the kingdom of God* (1 CORINTHIANS 6:9, 10).

We must resist the pressure to accept the arguments made for same-sex marriages heard daily on television and read in the newspapers. We must carefully expose the disinformation that has become so much a part of this debate. In fact, we as a church must become involved in the struggle to keep marriage according to God's intended program.

To this task we now turn.

The Church
Must Act

5

*We ignore the complete cultural impli-
cations of our faith. And then we're
shocked by the state of the culture.*

—CHARLES COLSON

WHILE THE WORD "MARRIAGE" is being redefined, we as a
Christian community seem to be asleep, perhaps believing
there is not much we can do, given the moral climate of our
times. The simple fact is that if we are not salt and light now,
we never will be.

But where do we begin?

We have to reopen the question of our responsibility as a
church to the wider culture. Should we retreat to our Bible
studies, or should we try to influence the present debate,
and if so, how shall we do it? Charles Colson says he was on
Capitol Hill recently and congressmen told him they are
alarmed over the lack of public support for the Federal
Marriage Amendment. Few calls and e-mails were coming in
over the issue. Colson asks: Are we asleep? He says, "We

ignore the complete cultural implications of our faith. And then we're shocked by the state of the culture."[1]

We might lose our battle to prevent same-sex marriages. There is little doubt that the culture, opinion polls notwithstanding, is ready to "live and let live" without any concern about the wider implications. In the midst of this, we must recover the notion of the church as a force for renewal rather than simply the agent of bitter confrontation. We must fight the war of values without compromising the only message that can change the hearts of men. If not, we are offering a temporary solution to what is in fact an eternal problem.

In ancient Rome, when the church was young and emperor worship was required of the citizenry at the pain of death, Christians understood that by calling Jesus *Lord*, they were entering the political world of their time. They could not afford to make a neat separation between their individual faith and their "public political philosophy." To refuse to deify Caesar was not just a religious question, but a political one as well. The Christian faith, rightly lived, has *always* collided with politics and popular culture.

After the 1925 Scopes trial, Christian fundamentalism retreated from meaningful involvement in our culture. The fundamentalist-modernist controversies made true believers withdraw, causing a sharp separation between our faith and culture. This vacuum created a popular moral and spiritual climate where values could be freely rewritten to conform to the irreligious spirit of the age. Christianity was still respected but also largely ignored. Christians formed a subculture that remained hidden to all except those who took the time to seek it out.

This retreat from meaningful involvement with the culture precipitated the erosion of values from the mainstream of America's social and political life. Obviously the Christian faith, isolated as it was, was not a threat to the gradual disintegration of the culture. The prevailing doctrine of separation from the world cut the church off from meaningful dialogue and influence with the world.

But we are learning that it is foolish to say that we can be wholly devoted to Jesus Christ in the private sphere, but we must not disturb the status quo in the public sphere. We must even be involved when our world becomes intolerant of common sense.

We must work both within the church and outside of it to influence the debate.

Our Responsibility Within the Church

As much as we might wish, there is no quick fix to stop the march toward same-sex marriages. But *we can have an impact*. We must think long-term, beginning with efforts that may not have immediate payoff but will yield great results in the future. Also, there are some things we can do outside the church that will have an eternal impact in the lives of many— and eventually change our cultural consensus toward a biblical worldview.

Let's Strengthen Our Families

For starters, let's begin with our own families. The statistics on divorce within the evangelical community are cause for repentance and shame. Christians, having drunk deeply from the cup of modernity, have opted for an escape clause in their marriage vows. Let us humbly confess that we have not modeled the virtues and values of family life for all the world to see.

ARE WE IN THE CHURCH WILLING TO MARRY ANY TWO PEOPLE AS LONG AS THEY CLAIM TO "LOVE EACH OTHER"? The fact that divorce continues rampant despite a spate of books on love, marriage, and the family, is a poignant reminder that our battle is not one of *information*, but *transformation*. Unless the heart is changed by the power of the gospel, we will never be the witness we should be to the world around us. We must be reminded that we can only move forward on our knees and in repentance and faith.

A few simple questions: Do we have adequate premarital and marital counseling in our churches, or are we willing to marry any two people as long as they claim to "love each other"? We as a church should not be in the business of marrying people, but rather in the business of establishing Christian marriages and Christian homes. When gays point to the statistics on divorce among heterosexuals, they make a telling point that we cannot ignore.

Second, we must lead the way in adoption. Yes, it is easy to criticize Rosie O'Donnell's decision to adopt a child; but Christian couples should be the first to step to the plate to adopt the precious children who deserve a mother and a father. Here, perhaps more than in any other matter, we need to put our actions where our mouths are. Consider, for example, the previously mentioned Calvary Chapel in Ft.

Lauderdale, Florida. Their involvement in adoption and foster care is an inspiring model.

Third, we must carefully nurture and protect our young people. Studies have shown that a child who reaches puberty can either become a homosexual or heterosexual depending on environmental factors.[2] Roger, a homosexual prostitute who converted to Christ and was later married told me, "I was introduced to homosexuality by a man across the street when I was about six years old. I both hated it and loved it; at last I had a man to turn to. Then when I reached the teen years, I just assumed I was gay and opted for the lifestyle." His story is one that can be repeated thousands of times.

We must stand against modern sex education curricula that suggest that young people "explore" their sexuality. Two Christian college girls who by their own testimony were heterosexual became enamored of lesbian pornography found on the Internet. They soon began to "experiment," acting out their fantasies. We should not wonder that they entered the lifestyle, living out the desires they had awakened.

I shall not enter into the debate about private vs. public schools except to say that parents must, at all costs, protect their children from those courses that will introduce their children to pornography under the guise of sex education and information that will encourage them to become sexually active. If we allow educators to "sexualize" our children, we lose our future. Worse, we have failed at the very point at which God holds us most responsible.

Let's Celebrate Singleness

We must realize that some of our young people think they might be gay because of sexual feelings for members of the same sex—some say that 25 percent of young boys question their sexuality at some point. They have awakened something within themselves that brings confusion and doubt. A boy might realize that he is different from other boys; he might cry more easily, be less athletic, and have an artistic temperament, provoking teasing from his peers. Unfortunately, given our pro-homosexual culture, such a young man will be encouraged to "experiment" and follow that lifestyle. This is dangerous in the extreme. If he begins such experimentation with a member of the same sex, he will overcome his reluctance to have these unnatural relationships. He will wrongly think he is gay and most likely pursue that lifestyle. The secrecy of it all not only plagues his conscience but fuels his desire.

In its strong condemnation of homosexuality, the church has failed to teach parents that children must not only be reared but *understood*. There is nothing wrong with a boy being effeminate; this, however, is not an indication that he was born a homosexual. The homosexual desires themselves are the result of environmental factors and a culture that insists that everyone has to be sexually active and "discover their gender." It might well be that such a young person will also be attracted to the opposite sex and discover that the struggles of puberty are a passing phase.

However, he might also have a special calling to singleness whereby he will serve the Lord.

When the disciples were overwhelmed with the level of commitment Jesus expected for marriage partners, they suggested that perhaps it was best if people not marry. And

Jesus made this statement, "For some are eunuchs because they were born that way; others were made that way by men; and others have renounced marriage because of the kingdom of heaven. The one who can accept this should accept it" (Matthew 19:12). A eunuch is generally defined as a castrated male who could be entrusted with a harem or a household. Jesus said that some are made that way by men; others, he says renounce marriage for the sake of the kingdom. But there is a first category: those who were "born that way." They are not called to marriage and family. God has other things in mind.

It is not too strong to say that we have made an idol of marriage. Singles are often asked, "Well, why aren't you married?" with the clear implication that there just might be something wrong with them and their singleness. We must stand against this insistence that marriage, with its sexual pleasures along with parental responsibilities, is best for everyone. We must realize that God Himself might have a calling for those who are single, either by necessity or by choice. We must celebrate singleness.

Let's Repent of Our Attitude

I've already said enough in this book about the need to minister to homosexuals without a spirit of judgmentalism or finger-pointing. I cannot stress too strongly that we must not view homosexuality as a sin that is divorced from our own sins within the church—adultery, greed, gossip, and pornography to name a few. Ed Dobson (no relation to James Dobson), senior pastor of a large church in Grand Rapids, received criticism when his church launched an outreach to gays several years ago. Some feared the church might be "overrun" with gays.

In *Leadership* journal Dobson replied, "If the church gets overrun with homosexuals, that will be terrific. They can take their place in the pews right next to the liars, gossips, materialists, and all the rest of us who entertain sin in our lives." He concludes by saying, "When I die, if someone stands up and says 'Ed Dobson loved homosexuals' then I will have accomplished something with my life."[3] No wonder homosexuals come to his church even though they know that he does not approve of their lifestyle.

If all that we have to offer the world is a message of judgment, we can understand why we will have lost the ear of those who need to hear us the most. I suspect that not many have left the gay lifestyle because they have heard a message condemning homosexuality. But many have left because of a message of hope, grace, and patience.

The world is intolerant of hypocrites—those who condemn others for doing what they themselves do in secret. Credibility with our neighbors and friends can best be nurtured through a spirit of openness, admitting our own struggles and short-comings. If you want to find a bridge to witness of Christ to your neighbors, share some of your failures with them. They will be quite pleased to know that you, as a Christian, are not exempt from the failings common to man.

FIGHTING LIKE CHRIST

There are two dangers we must avoid at this hour. The first is to retreat from the fray because we believe that in the end gay marriages will be legalized, and thus "whatever will be will be." Years ago, in a letter to his supporters, James Dobson pointed out that even if evangelicals choose to run and hide, they will not be able to do so indefinitely. He asked: At what point will we be willing to defend what we believe? Will parents object if their children are routinely indoctrinated in homosexual ideology or occultism in the public schools? Will we object if the state tells us as pastors what we can (or can't) say from the pulpit? Such a specter is not so unimaginable. In Sweden an evangelical pastor who preached a sermon on Sodom and Gomorrah was convicted of "verbal violence" against homosexuals and sentenced to a four-week prison term.

Recall that Queen Esther thought she would be safe if she remained silent in the court of the evil king Ahasuerus even though the Jews were about to be persecuted. But her cousin Mordecai perceptively said, "Think not with thyself that thou shalt escape in the king's house, more than all the Jews. . . . And who knoweth whether thou art come to the kingdom for such a time as this?" (Esther 4:13–14, KJV). Fearfully, but obediently, she spoke to the king, and disaster was averted.

JOHN Q. CITIZEN WILL NEVER BE CONVINCED ABOUT THE CREDIBILITY OF THE CHRISTIAN FAITH UNTIL HE BECOMES PERSONALLY ACQUAINTED WITH SOMEONE WHO LIVES OUT THE CHRISTIAN LIFE.

We've been brought to the kingdom for such a time as this, and we cannot run and hide. We cannot retreat. Even if same-sex marriages should be legalized, we must still press the issues working toward a Federal Marriage Amendment and working toward a change in the collective national mood.

The second danger we must avoid is to become so involved in our same-sex marriage debate that we forget that the primary message we have for the world is that Jesus died on the cross for sinners. We are to be agents of grace, mercy and forgiveness in a harsh and cruel world. We cannot let our cultural revolution obscure our primary calling. We must exercise that calling *within the context of our cultural debate*.

How can we meaningfully be engaged in a massive cultural and moral struggle without diverting the attention of the world from its need for faith in Christ? Since the answer cannot be to retreat, we must fight; but we must fight like Christians—or more accurately, we must fight like Christ. We have responsibilities in three areas.

What Can I Do?

We thank God for the Christian media; but at least for the foreseeable future, the secular media will not help us. We can no longer expect to call this nation back to God by public outcries. We cannot appeal to a "moral majority" when, in fact, none exists.

There is, in my opinion, only one answer: Every single Christian must become an activist, assuming the delicate task of taking a firm but loving stand on the issues and yet presenting the spiritual healing of Christ to a society afflicted with a disease called sin. John Q. Citizen will never be convinced about the credibility of the Christian faith until he becomes personally acquainted with someone who lives out the Christian life, applying its values to every situation.

Many Americans think they don't know anyone personally who is a born-again Christian; they don't know anyone who is pro-life and yet loves women who have had an abortion.

Nor have they met someone opposed to same-sex marriages who does not hate homosexuals. They have never met anyone who would oppose an occult curriculum in the public schools and yet be a genuinely caring individual. In fact they likely know such a person but he or she has remained silent for fear of being thought of as a fanatic or a religious nut.

The church must begin today to equip believers to lovingly live out their values in neighborhoods, hospitals, factories, and business offices of this land. Only one-on-one can we model the love of Christ and change the misrepresentations that are perpetrated almost daily by the media. Credibility *at* the grassroots of American life can only be restored *by* the grassroots. Only you and I personally can move the debate to higher ground.

Those who are not on the front lines of battle are not exempt from conflict. Parents whose children are grown, or those who work in vocations seemingly unaffected by the clash of values, must be enlisted. During World War II, it was estimated that for every person on the front lines there were twenty who provided the support systems. We cannot leave the battle to those who are dodging bullets in the trenches.

Older parents must stand with younger ones whose children are subjected to pro-homosexual teachings in the schools. Christian college students must rally their peers who are being discriminated against because they do not accept the politically correct liberal agenda. Every believer must be willing to come to the aid of another, bridging all age, vocational, economic, and racial barriers. No one should feel that he or she is in this conflict alone.

We must overcome our reluctance to make our views known in our neighborhoods, at work, and among our friends. We cannot be followers of Christ and consider our reputation to be of more value than standing for the Christ who has saved us. We cannot be intimidated by frivolous lawsuits, harassment on the job, or even death threats. The lordship of Christ means just that: He is our one and only Lord.

When we are misrepresented, we must respond as Christ did: He refused to lash out in anger and did not resort to dramatic outbursts of power to "even the score." He confronted His accusers with truth, yet remained fully in control of His responses. He knew that conflict with evil men was God's plan for Him.

Like Queen Esther, we have all come to the kingdom for such a time as this. We must stand for truth at every level and yet realize that what men and women need most is to see Jesus. A full mind is powerful only when combined with a changed heart.

What Can We Do?

Just as we must cross denominational lines in our fight against abortion, so we must gladly reach out to those who agree with our stand against same-sex marriages despite other doctrinal differences. The battle for traditional marriage has brought together Catholics and Protestants, Hispanics and African-Americans, Baptists and Pentecostals and Reformed believers, such as Fuller Seminary president Richard Mouw, who calls efforts to redefine marriage "dangerously sinful." He's right—and all of us, despite our other differences, need to stand together.

Thankfully, many excellent resources have been developed to help believers stand for biblical values in every level of society. There are grassroots organizations that have had experience in networking action groups that can have a collective witness for Christ while addressing the issues that affect a given community. We can be grateful for organizations such as Focus on the Family, Concerned Women for America, and the Family Research Council. We support the Massachusetts Family Institute that has mounted opposition to the decision of the state Supreme Court to approve same-sex marriages. The Alliance for Marriage is working as an umbrella organization to help to retain traditional marriage and promote a constitutional amendment defining marriage as between one man and one woman. The American Center for Law and Justice keeps putting pressure on the courts to keep rogue judges from inventing new laws. These groups and others like them need our prayers and our support. No one organization can do it alone. This is not a matter of competition, but uniting for the common good of our country.

In the midst of this, we must not allow differences of opinion or strategy to divide us. For example, some evangelicals have come out in support of civil unions for gays, which would give gays some of the benefits of marriage but still reserve marriage for heterosexual couples. The risk of this, of course, is that heterosexuals might also opt for such an arrangement as they have in France and Sweden. Ron Crews of the Massachusetts Family Institute said, "[The issue of] civil unions is merely marriage by another name and devalues the institution of marriage."[4] What is more, he says, some business owners wouldn't want to provide benefits for same-sex partners on moral grounds. Yes, same-sex unions are marriage by another name.

David Midwood of Vision New England, a multicultural Christian coalition, suggests a middle way. He supports some kind of a "domestic partnership" that would be applicable even for nonsexual relationships such as an aged mother being taken care of by her child. These partnerships would be for health insurance and property rights.[5] These matters must be debated among us, but we cannot lose focus as we address the immediate issue of same-sex marriages. Politically speaking, we sometimes have to be satisfied with a half-loaf rather than none at all.

Does Voting Matter?

As a minister I believe strongly that neither my church nor I should endorse a political candidate, even if he or she is a Christian. We all know how disappointing Christians can be once they are in office. The lure of political pressure and need for reelection have often caused even the best politicians to compromise important convictions.

That said, I think it is critically important that as individual citizens we work within the political arena to elect those who are favorable to a pro-family agenda, in opposing abortion and same-sex marriages. We must find those politicians at all levels who are willing to articulate their views and know what we expect of them once in office. We must even try to educate them and their assistants in why a particular stand is important.

As individuals we must exercise all the influence we have with letters, e-mails, and phone calls to our politicians to help them understand their constituency. Colson writes, "What will it take to awaken the Church? What's it going to take for all of you good people listening and reading today to get on the telephones to call your congressman, senators and state legislators to say, 'We want to protect marriage'?"[6]

We all know that every president's future influence is found in the appointing of judges who in turn affect public policy sometimes for decades to come. Indeed, the present trend is to bypass democracy and let activist judges dictate policy, based on personal preference and arbitrary power. We must have a groundswell of objections to these developments.

OUR PRIMARY JOB IS NOT TO SAVE AMERICA. OUR RESPONSIBILITY IS TO STAND FOR CHRIST, WITNESSING TO HIS GRACE AND POWER.

Yes, politics matters.

His Healing, His Power

However, we must realize that ultimately the same-sex marriage debate is not a matter simply of politics, nor a matter of judicial activism. At root is the spiritual emptiness of a nation that has turned from God and lost its way.

A growing number of people are beginning to realize that our problems are not merely political, economic, racial, or even moral. Unless we find a remedy for the human spirit, our downward spiral will accelerate. The Gospel of our triumphant Christ is the only answer.

Our primary job is not to save America. Our first responsibility is not to preserve our freedoms, important though they are. Our responsibility is to stand for Christ, witnessing to His grace and power. Our lives should rectify the false notions that persist about Him. Those of us who have experienced Christ's healing must bring His power to a society that has concluded that no cure for its ills exists. Our neighbors have to know that we are not their enemies, but their truest friends.

The churches to whom Peter wrote were islands of righteousness in a sea of paganism. He encouraged them with these words, "Dear friends, do not be surprised at the painful trial you are suffering, as though something strange were happening to you. But rejoice that you participate in the sufferings of Christ, so that you may be overjoyed when his glory is revealed. If you are insulted because of the name of Christ, you are blessed, for the Spirit of glory and of God rests on you" (1 Peter 4:12–14).

Yet one more challenge awaits.

We Must Seek God

6

"We do not know what to do, but our eyes are upon you."

—2 Chronicles 20:12

IT'S GONE.

Remember when Francis Schaeffer told us that some day we would wake up and find out the America we once knew was gone? *That day is here.*

We have crossed an invisible line, and there are no signs that we are capable of turning back. Like a boat caught in the mighty torrent of the Niagara River, we are being swept along in a powerful cultural current that just might pull us over the brink.

Daily, perhaps hourly, we seem to be losing the war for America's heart and mind. We must understand the direction and speed of this cultural river that has spilled over and engulfed our land. Even though a majority of Americans oppose same-sex marriages, we might have centuries of laws overturned, not by the electorate but by judicial fiat. The battle is waged in our courtrooms, independent of the input of our citizenry.

On several occasions I've been in the so-called Luther Room in the Wartburg Castle in Germany. There, living the life of a hermit, Luther translated the entire New Testament into German in just ten months! But it is also there, tradition says, he threw an inkwell at the devil. Indeed, tour guides used to rub a bit of soot on the wall, because tourists wanted to see where the inkwell landed!

If Luther did indeed throw his inkwell at the devil I'm sure that the devil was not perturbed. No evil spirit would fear an inkwell coming in his direction, even if it were thrown with accuracy and speed. No demon would duck, hoping it would miss its target. You can't fight a spiritual being with physical weapons! Physical battles are fought with physical weapons, spiritual battles with spiritual weapons.

As I emphasized in the last chapter, we must use the opportunities at our disposal to stand against same-sex unions. We must do so individually and we must support pro-family organizations. We must and should become involved politically. But these methods just might be missing their intended target. Such measures might do much better than an inkwell thrown at the devil, but they in themselves will not reverse our cultural current.

The average evangelical thinks that God will always be on our side in our battle against same-sex marriage. However, in the Old Testament, God said these startling words to His chosen people: "Yet they rebelled and grieved his Holy Spirit. So he turned and became their enemy, and he himself fought against them" (Isaiah 63:10). In other words, there are times when God no longer takes up the cause of His people. When we refuse to repent of our own sins, God might refuse to come to our aid and let us be defeated. This is why we must turn to Him as families, as churches, and as individuals. Without repentance for our own sins, we cannot expect to win our cultural wars. I believe very deeply that only God can save us now.

Of course, we have always believed that only God can save us. But never have we needed His intervention so desperately; never before have we felt so helpless in the face of a massive national movement that it appears we cannot stop. And millions of middle-of-the-road Americans who have nothing to do with gays and the gay movement are lulled by the media rhetoric and misrepresentation. They think that we can "live and let live" as if homosexual marriages can exist alongside of traditional ones, each staying in their separate section of the boat we call America.

Ours is a battle than cannot be won by reason, scientific data, or dialogue. The radical homosexual movement that preaches tolerance will not itself tolerate alternate opinions. Everyone must move in lockstep with their agenda—or pay a price.

One day the king Jehoshaphat woke up and was told that a vast army was coming against him. The king consulted God about what to do and proclaimed a fast throughout the land of Judah. The people then gathered from every town in the land to seek help from the Lord. Jehoshaphat then stood in the temple of the Lord, and prayed.

> *O LORD, God of our fathers, are you not the God who is in heaven? You rule over all the kingdoms of the nations. Power and might are in your hand, and no one can withstand you. O our God, did you not drive out*

the inhabitants of this land before your people Israel and give it forever to the descendants of Abraham your friend? . . . If calamity comes upon us, whether the sword of judgment, or plague or famine, we will stand in your presence before this temple that bears your Name and will cry out to you in our distress, and you will hear and save us. . . . O our God, will you not judge them [the adversaries]? For we have no power to face this vast army that is attacking us. We do not know what to do, but our eyes are upon you (2 CHRONICLES 20:6–7; 9; 12, EMPHASIS ADDED).

We do not know what to do, but our eyes are upon you!

I wonder what would happen if millions of believers set aside their schedules to seek God on behalf of this nation. . . .

I wonder what would happen if privately and corporately we confessed our sins and turned away from our own idols. . . .

I wonder if perhaps God would intervene so the destruction of marriage and the forces that seek to tear our families apart would be stayed.

Back to Jehoshaphat: Through a man anointed with the Spirit, the word of the Lord came, "Do not be afraid or discouraged because of this vast army. For the battle is not yours but God's"(v. 15). Then the king commanded that a select group of men walk ahead of the army singing and praising God for the splendor of His holiness. And God gave the victory!

Eighteenth-century Britain was in such a state of decline that Parliament had to be dismissed in the middle of the day because too many of the members were in a drunken stupor. Children were abandoned to die and immorality was rampant. The knowledge of God had all but faded from view.

Mercifully, God reversed that trend through the preaching of John Wesley and George Whitefield. Some historians believe that it was that revival that spared Britain the bloody fate of France, torn by violent revolution.

Please understand that God does not owe us such a deliverance. No nation has turned away from so much light in order to choose darkness. No nation has squandered as many opportunities as we have. We can only call on God for mercy, and if it please Him He will come to our aid. We certainly cannot expect a revival simply because we do not want to face the harassment that well might come to us all. But if we humble ourselves, weeping for this nation, God may yet intervene and restore decency to this crazed world. Most of all, we should pray that millions would be converted and belong to God forever. People change their minds only when God changes their hearts.

If we cannot weep before God, we are probably not fit to fight before men.

Only He can save us now.

NOTES

While We Were Sleeping . . .

1. Lynn Vincent, "Remaking the American Family," *World*, 6 March 2004:18.

2. Ibid.

3. Ibid.

4. Jeffrey Satinover, *Homosexuality and the Politics of Truth* (Grand Rapids: Baker Books, 1996), 33.

5. *Psychiatric Annals*, April 1976.

6. Alan Sears and Craig Osten, *The Homosexual Agenda: Exposing the Principal Threat to Religious Freedom Today* (Nashville: Broadman and Holman, 2003), 18. I encourage you to read this well-documented book that deals with a wide scope of gay agenda issues.

7. Ibid., 22.

8. Ibid., 21, 22.

9. Ibid., 23.

10. Ibid., 8, footnote.

11. Ibid., 26, 27.

12. Ibid., 26.

13. Ibid., 48.

Chapter 1: The Church Must Speak

1. Alan Sears and Craig Osten, *The Homosexual Agenda: Exposing the Principal Threat to Religious Freedom Today* (Nashville: Broadman and Holman, 2003), 52.

2. Ibid., 92.

3. Ibid.

4. Ibid., 90.

5. Ibid., 93.

6. Ibid., 94.

7. Ibid.

8. Ibid., 95.

9. Joel Belz, "A Totally Alien Mindset," *World*, 20 March 2004: n/p.

10. Ibid.

11. Jeffrey Satinover, *Homosexuality and the Politics of Truth* (Grand Rapids: Baker Books, 1996), 36.

12. Ibid.

13. John Leo, "Stomping on Free Speech," 12 April 2004, http://*Townhall.com*

14. Richard Roeper, "Good to see the president has his priorities in order," *Chicago Sun-Times*, 25 February 2004: 11.

15. James R. White and Jeffrey D. Niell, *The Same-Sex Controversy* (Minneapolis: Bethany House, 2002). This is a valuable resource in exposing the fallacies of interpretation that seek to neutralize the biblical teaching about homosexuality.

16. Sears and Osten, *Agenda*, 13.

Chapter 2: We Must Consult the Designer's Manual

1. Quoted in Tim Alan Gardner, *Sacred Sex* (Colorado Springs, Colo.: WaterBrook Press, 2002), 38.

2. Ibid., 16.

3. P. Roger Hillerstrom, *Intimate Deception* (Portland, Ore.: Multnomah, 1989), 30.

4. Quoted in Gardner, 23.

Chapter 3: We Must Remember the Children

1. The *Windy City Times*, 24 March 2004: 10.

2. Alan Sears and Craig Osten, *The Homosexual Agenda: Exposing the Principal Threat to Religious Freedom Today* (Nashville: Broadman and Holman, 2003), 68, 69.

3. Christian Coalition International (Canada), Inc. http://ccicinc.org.

4. Ibid.

5. Ibid.

6. Christianity Today Online, "Would a Marriage by Any Other Name Be the Same?" 8 March 2004, http://christianitytoday.com.

7. Ibid.

8. Hillary Rodham Clinton, *It Takes a Village—and Other Lessons Children Teach Us* (New York: Touchstone, 1996), 50.

9. Tammy Bruce, *The Death of Right and Wrong* (California: Forum, An Imprint of Prima Publishing, 2003), 87.

10. Ibid., 88.

11. Ibid., 195.

12. C. Everett Koop and Francis Schaeffer, *Whatever Happened to the Human Race?* rev. ed. (Wheaton, Ill.: Crossway Books, 1983), 2.

13. Ibid., 3.

14. "Gay lawmaker testifies: 'Who are we hurting?'"*Chicago Tribune*, 24 March 2004: 11.

15. *The Family Research Report*, Vol. 18, No. 8, December 2003.

Chapter 4: We Must Resist the Pressure

1. Stanton L. Jones and Mark A. Yarhouse, *Homosexuality: The Use of Scientific Research in the Church's Moral Debate* (Downers Grove, Ill.: InterVarsity Press, 2000), 48.

2. Ibid., 51.

3. Ibid., 73 ff.

4. Ibid., 89.

5. Ibid., 90.

6. Ibid., 117.

7. Ibid., 149.

8. Ibid., 150.

9. Dwight A. McBride, "Racism among homosexuals and homophobia among blacks,"*Chicago Tribune*, 28 March 2004: 7.

10. Jones and Yarhouse, the footnote on 167.

11. Dennis Prager, "Who Supports Same-Sex Marriage?" 9 March 2004, http://*Townhall.com*.

12. Jones and Yarhouse, 149, 150.

13. Ibid., 110.

14. *Family Research Report*, Vol. 18 No. 8, December 2003.

15. Timothy Dailey, Ph. D., "Comparing the Lifestyles of Homosexual Couples to Married Couples," 29 April 2004, http://*frc.org*.

Chapter 5: The Church Must Act

1. Charles Colson, "BreakPoint" commentary, 13 April 2004.

2. For excellent scientific information about the causes of homosexuality, see the website http://*narth.com*. (More information on the "Resources" page.)

3. Tim Stafford, "Ed Dobson Loves Homosexuals," *Christianity Today*, 19 July 1993, from online archives (http://*christianitytoday.com*). Dobson's Church, Calvary Baptist, and its "Gen. X"-oriented church plant, Mars Hill Bible Church, continue to minister to those struggling with such issues..

4. Tony Carnes, "Amending Marriage," *Christianity Today*, April 2004: 92.

5. Ibid.

6. Colson, "BreakPoint" commentary.

Resources

Whether you have a friend or family member struggling with homosexuality, wish to learn more about the same-sex marriage debate, or want to help promote biblical values in our culture, there is a wealth of resources available. Here are some of the best:

National Association for Research and Therapy of Homosexuality (*www.narth.com*)

This organization was founded by professionals in the fields of psychiatry and psychology. They state: "As mental-health professionals, we need a full and complete understanding of homosexuality." Their website offers a wide variety of resources, book reviews, articles, research updates, and perspectives on such topics as "reparative" therapy, which seeks to help homosexuals leave their lifestyle). Parents of young people wondering if they're gay will find much help here and in founder Joseph Nicolosi's book *A Parent's Guide to Preventing Homosexuality* (InterVarsity Press, 2002).

BreakPoint (*www.pfm.org*)

Charles Colson's "BreakPoint" commentaries on faith and contemporary culture are widely heard on Christian radio. This section of his Prison Fellowship website includes commentaries, resources and more. They offer a "Speak the Truth in Love Resource Kit," designed to help Christians share a compassionate, biblical perspective with gay loved ones.

Focus on the Family (*www.family.org*)

This is the organization that, more than any other, brought issues of family and society to the attention of the church. An excellent and helpful website.

Family Research Council (*www.frc.org*)

FRC is primarily an advocacy group that monitors developments in Washington and nationwide. They have been very active in the marriage debates.

Alliance for Marriage (*www.allianceformarriage.org*)

AFM is spearheading the constitutional amendment that would define "marriage" as being between a man and a woman. Their motto is "More Children Raised in a Home With a Mother and Father."

Institute for Marriage and Public Policy (*www.marriagedebate.com*)

Maggie Gallagher, author of the well-received book *The Case for Marriage*, heads this organization. The website provides numerous links, updates, and perspectives on the significance of marriage in general and the current same-sex marriage controversies.

About the Author

Since 1980, Erwin W. Lutzer has served as senior pastor of the world-famous Moody Church in Chicago, where he provides leadership to Chicago pastors. A renowned theologian, Dr. Lutzer earned his B.Th. from Winnipeg Bible College, a Th.M. from Dallas Theological Seminary, an M.A. in philosophy from Loyola University, an LL.D. from Simon Greenleaf School of Law, and a D.D. from Western Conservative Baptist Seminary.

Dr. Lutzer is the featured speaker on three radio programs, including "The Moody Church Hour," the popular evening program "Songs in the Night," as well as the daily broadcast called "Running to Win." These programs are available on the Moody Broadcasting Network and are heard on hundreds of Christian radio stations around the country.

Dr. Lutzer is the author of numerous books, including *The Vanishing Power of Death*, *Cries from the Cross*, the best-selling *One Minute Before You Die*, and *Hitler's Cross*, which received the Evangelical Christian Publishers Association (ECPA) Gold Medallion Book Award. He speaks both nationally and internationally at Bible conferences and seminars and has led tours of the cities of the Protestant Reformation in Europe.

Dr. Lutzer and his wife, Rebecca, live in the Chicago area and are the parents of three grown children.

Acknowledgments

This book could not have been written without help and encouragement from many people. Special thanks to Greg Thornton and Bill Thrasher for challenging me to do the project; without your insistence I would not have undertaken this interesting challenge. Mark Tobey and Betsey Newenhuyse are to be thanked for helping me with research materials that were critical in writing the book. And Betsey, your creative editing not only corrected my grammar but your helpful changes made the book more readable. My administrative assistant, Patti Broderick, cleared my schedule and kept the lines of communication open in my office during particularly busy times. Without your help, Patti, I could not have given this project the attention it needed.

Finally, I thank my dear wife, Rebecca, who, believing in the importance of this work, was willing to put up with my long hours at the computer. Without your love, prayers, and support, Rebecca, my writing career would have come to a halt long ago.

Let all who read this book know it could only be done with the cooperation of all who faithfully work at Moody Publishers and are committed to the propagation of God's Word throughout the world. May we always represent Christ with wisdom and grace. And in all things we give thanks to God for the privilege of loving and serving Him in our fallen world.

MORE TITLES FROM ERWIN LUTZER

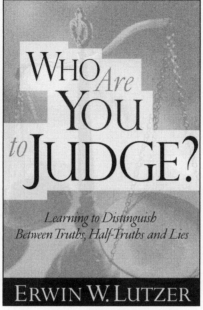

ISBN: 0-8024-0906-7

Who Are You to Judge?

Our task is to make wise judgments in a non-judgmental world!

Who Are You to Judge? is a book about discernment: the ability to distinguish the false from the true, or better, the false from the half-true. Erwin Lutzer helps Christians distinguish biblical Christianity from counterfeit spirituality.

Who Are You to Judge? *reminds us that truth is important, and (contrary to the spirit of our age) real truth is not merely a matter of subjective individual opinion.*

—JOHN MACARTHUR, PASTOR-TEACHER,
GRACE COMMUNITY CHURCH

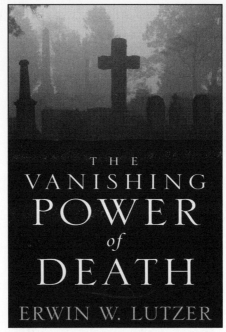

ISBN: 0-8024-0944-X

The Vanishing Power of Death

Christ's early followers scoffed at death, calling it a tyrant who had been overthrown by Christ. They knew that the end of their earthly life was a glorious beginning, and that the best was yet to come.

Can we believe the same? Absolutely! Dr. Lutzer unfolds the glorious implications of Jesus' death and resurrection, showing how we need not fear the grave, because Christ has crushed the enemy.

Ideal for personal or group study!

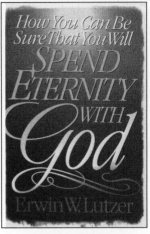

ISBN: 0-8024-2719-7

How You Can Be Sure That You Will Spend Eternity with God

You can know with certainty where you will be after death. Erwin Lutzer insists that many who expect to enter heaven will discover that they were sadly mistaken.

It is not too late for those who are still living to choose the right path and know it!

Perfect resource for seekers and new believers!

One Minute After You Die

One minute after you die, you will either be enjoying a personal welcome from your Savior or catching your first glimpse of gloom as you have never known it. Erwin Lutzer peels back the veil of this often misunderstood subject and lets the lamp of Scripture light the way.

Ideal for loved ones facing terminal illness or for comforting grieving family members.

ISBN: 0-8024-6322-3

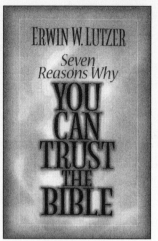

ISBN: 0-8024-8439-5

Seven Reasons Why You Can Trust the Bible

God has left us a single, trust-worthy source that reveals who He is. Erwin Lutzer gives seven compelling reasons we can trust the Bible using arguments from logic, personal experience, history and even science. This could be the single most important book you may ever read.

Cries from the Cross

The crucifixion of Jesus Christ brings us face to face with two seemingly contrary attributes of God—His love and His wrath, with two seemingly contradic-tory doctrines—the sovereignty of God and the free will of man. Once we under-stand Calvary, we can understand what it is to deny ourselves, take up our cross daily and follow Him. This is a work we should all read.

—KAY ARTHUR
PRECEPT MINISTRIES

ISBN: 0-8024-1111-8

MOODY
PUBLISHERS
THE NAME YOU CAN TRUST®

1-800-678-6928 · www.MoodyPublishers.org

Sɪɴᴄᴇ 1894, Moody Publishers has been dedicated to equip and motivate people to advance the cause of Christ by publishing evangelical Christian literature and other media for all ages, around the world. As a ministry of the Moody Bible Institute of Chicago, proceeds from the sale of this book help to train the next generation of Christian leaders.

If we may serve you in any way in your spiritual journey toward understanding Christ and the Christian life, please contact us at www.moodypublishers.com.

"All Scripture is God-breathed and is useful for teaching, rebuking, correcting and training in righteousness, so that the man of God may be thoroughly equipped for every good work."
—2 Tɪᴍᴏᴛʜʏ 3:16, 17

MOODY
PUBLISHERS
THE NAME YOU CAN TRUST®

The Truth About Same-Sex Marriage Team

ACQUIRING EDITOR
Greg Thornton

DEVELOPMENTAL EDITORS
Elizabeth Cody Newenhuyse
Mark Tobey

BACK COVER COPY
Elizabeth Cody Newenhuyse

COVER DESIGN
Paetzold Associates

INTERIOR DESIGN
Paetzold Associates

PRINTING AND BINDING
Dickinson Press Inc.

The typeface for the text of this book is
Palatino

Churches!

Save 50%

on a caselot* or more of

The Truth About Same-Sex Marriage

Ask your local retailer about having cases shipped directly to you for as low as $3.99 (U.S.) a book. Or call 1-800-678-6928.

* Each case contains 36 books

www.marriageofsamesex.com

Churches!

Christian Jr./Sr High School
2100 Greenfield Dr
El Cajon, CA 92019

See Multiple Purchase Special

on the reverse page.